THE
BEST OF BACON
·C·O·O·K·B·O·O·K·

THE
BEST OF BACON
·C·O·O·K·B·O·O·K·

EDITED BY MARY NORWAK & EMMA MANDERSON

OVER 150 TRADITIONAL RECIPES
AND NEW IDEAS

QUILLER PRESS
LONDON

Conceived and originated by the Dutch Meat Board

First published in 1987 by
Quiller Press Ltd
50 Albemarle Street
London W1X 4BD

Designed and produced by Roger Walker/Linde Hardaker
Photography by David Johnson
Illustrations by Alison Wisenfeld
Food styling by Kit Johnson
Food preparation by Lynn Rutherford
Bacon supplied by the Dutch Meat Board

ISBN 0 907621 84 8

Filmset by Katerprint Typesetting Services, Oxford
Printed and bound in Great Britain by Butler & Tanner,
Frome, Somerset.

Frontispiece
Tartlet filled with scrambled egg and bacon,
prawns wrapped in bacon with corn salad,
ham in parsley jelly

CONTENTS

ACKNOWLEDGEMENTS

The publishers would like to thank Trusthouse Forte for providing original recipes from head chefs throughout their hotel group; also Caroline Liddell and Heidi Lascelles of Books for Cooks, for their generous help during research.

Quiller Press gratefully acknowledges the following publishers who have given permission to reproduce recipes:

Allen Lane, for baked ham crusted with ground almonds and hymettus honey, from Michael Smith's *Homes and Gardens Cookbook*; Batsford, for devilled kidneys in bacon, from Anne Willan's *Entertaining*; Collins, for Cumberland bacon and egg pie, from Michael Smith's *A Cook's Tour of Britain*; The Dovecote Press, for Wiltshire bacon scones, from Angela Rawson and Nikki Kedge's *Wiltshire Cookery*; Granada, for bacon olives in lemon sauce, and barbecue relish, from Carol Wright's *Complete Meat Cookery*; Hutchinson, for *rigodon bourgignon*, and *pounti*, from Anne Willan's *French Regional Cooking*; IPC Magazines, for prawns wrapped in bacon with a corn salad by Nigel Slater, and little gammon and artichoke pies, by Philippa Davenport, both from *A La Carte*; Macmillan, for an adaptation of carrot and spinach mousses, from Anton Mosimann's *Cuisine Naturelle*; Michael Joseph, for gammon with pineapple, from *Jane Grigson's Fruit Book*, and stuffed cabbage leaves Limoges style, from *Jane Grigson's Vegetable Book*; Octopus, for cheese-topped gammon, from *Good Housekeeping Cooking for Today*; Orbis, for ham fritters, from Valerie-Anne l'Etoile, Monique Maine and Madeleine Peter's *La Cuisine*; Penguin, for ham croquettes, from Jane Grigson's *Charcuterie and French Pork Cookery, brithyll a cig moch*, from Jane Grigson's *Fish Cookery*, and scalloped ham with mushrooms and cheese, from Jane Grigson's *The Mushroom Feast*; Reader's Digest, for gammon steaks with Madeira sauce, from *The Cookery Year*; Sainsbury's, for treacle baked collar of bacon, baked bacon joint with red beans and spiced apples, and ham rolls stuffed with turkey breast in a spinach sauce, from *The Josceline Dimbleby Collection*, and Scandinavian mustard sauce, from Anne Willan's *Sauces, Marinades and Dressings*; World's Work, for sour cream and bacon pancakes with melon, from Ingeborg Pertwee's *For Starters*.

INTRODUCTION

The British have been eating bacon for nearly 2000 years since the Roman occupation, and it has always been one of our most popular foods. Country people used to keep a family pig to eat their scraps and feed them through the year, and the pig has always been considered a symbol of thrift and prosperity. Meat had to be salted in former years as animals could not easily be fed during the winter months, and even in these modern times we still retain our taste for this flavoursome meat.

The most significant development in the UK bacon market over the past few years has been the great increase in the Dutch share. The Dutch are fortunate in that their pig is heavier and more mature, with a large eye of meat content in its lean-to-fat ratio that makes it particularly good for cooking, whether as skinless defatted bacon or rind-on bacon. Having given strong attention to the processing of this raw material, that is a quality-guaranteed product known as Dutch Royal Crest, they are determined to see bacon take its place in a wider cuisine.

Bacon is incredibly versatile, whether served as rashers or steaks, or in the form of joints or splendid hams. Bacon may be used for every meal of the day, from the nourishing cooked breakfast through the light lunch and simple snack to the comforting supper and the full-blown dinner party or buffet, not forgetting all those tasty teas, happy picnics and handy sandwiches in between.

The most amateur cook can produce a delicious meal with bacon, but the experienced and creative one can prepare a wonderful range of dishes with bacon's natural partners – all kinds of fruit and vegetables, herbs and spices, beer and cider, and even fish and seafood. This book aims to show you just a mere 150 recipes based on the best of ingredients – Bacon.

CHOOSING AND BUYING BACON

Today's bacon may be bought in neatly labelled packs so that the customer can see exactly what is available in the quantity she needs. The housewife is now looking for leaner, tastier bacon without excessive saltiness, which provides value for money and nourishment for the family, whether she is buying rashers or joints. Dutch bacon scores highly on all these counts.

Streaky rashers combine lean and fat and may be grilled or fried, when the fat will become crisp. Streaky bacon is useful for chopping into soups and casseroles, for flavouring pasta, and for lining pâté dishes.

Back rashers are lean and may be grilled or fried. They are useful in recipes which require flavour without additional fat.

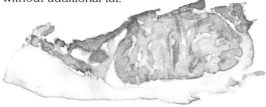

Middlecut rashers combine back and streaky bacon and may be used for grilling or frying, or in recipes.

Bacon steaks are thick rashers which may be grilled or fried, but which lend themselves to sophisticated dishes when paired with sauces, pulses or fruit garnishes. *Gammon steaks* are cut from the leg (ham) and are large and lean and very suitable for entertaining dishes.

Bacon joints may be small enough for a single family meal, or large enough for a big party. *Collar* and *forehock* are small joints with a good mixture of lean and fat, and these are excellent for boiling or braising, or they may be cubed for casseroles. *Butt* is the leanest part, best boiled. *Small hock* is good for mincing and casseroling. *Fore slipper* is less lean, a tasty piece for boiling.

Top Fore slipper
Below Small hock
Right Butt

The prime joints are from the rear leg or 'ham' of the animal. A full ham can weigh up to 30 lb/15 kg, but a half ham is a more manageable size for the average party. *Middle gammon* from the upper leg makes a smaller joint for a party, and is lean and meaty. *Gammon hock* from the lower leg is a good shape for boiling or baking with a glaze, and a *Corner Gammon* is a triangular joint which is useful for the same purpose. *Gammon slipper* is a small, lean joint for boiling.

Above, left to right
Gammon hock, middle gammon, corner gammon
Below Gammon slipper

STORAGE

Bacon is best kept in the refrigerator, and the pack will give a date for the expiry of shelf-life. When a pack has been opened, it should be treated as fresh bacon, and used up within 7 days (refrigerator) or 4 days (cool larder).

Vacuum-packed bacon may be kept in the freezer, although there is little point in keeping it this way except for emergency use· on return from holidays. Salted meat with fat has a short storage life before flavour changes occur. Smoked and unsmoked joints will keep up to 4 months; smoked and unsmoked rashers and bacon steaks up to 3 months.

INTRODUCTION

NUTRITION

Bacon is a highly nutritious food which is rich in protein. A 4 oz/100 g gammon steak contains 16.8 per cent protein compared to 17.5 for a 4 oz/100 g cod steak and only 9 per cent for $\frac{1}{2}$ pint/300 ml milk and 6.8 for 1 egg. There is no appreciable amount of carbohydrate in bacon. It is a valuable source of the important B group vitamins, particularly thiamin (vitamin B_1) – cooked bacon contains four times as much thiamin as the same weight of beef or lamb. Since bacon is such a good companion to so many other types of food, it encourages us to eat good things like potatoes, pulses, wholemeal bread, fruit and vegetables which give a balanced diet.

COOKING BACON

Bacon is very easy to cook but careful selection of cuts and accurate timing will give best results.

GRILLING   Gives a delicious result and allows excess fat to drain away from the bacon. Thick rashers or steaks should be derinded, or the fat snipped to prevent curling during cooking. The bacon should be cooked until the fat becomes transparent.
Cuts to use Streaky, back and middlecut rashers; gammon steaks.

FRYING   No extra fat is necessary for frying bacon. The rashers should be arranged in a cold pan, overlapping lean over fat. The heat should be low for soft bacon and hotter for crisp bacon. Lift bacon out of the pan carefully to drain off excess fat, and use this fat for frying eggs, bread, tomatoes or mushrooms.
Cuts to use Streaky, back and middlecut rashers; gammon steaks.

BOILING   Bacon should never be 'boiled' but cooked very gently so that the liquid only just bubbles. Weigh the bacon joint and allow 20 minutes per lb/450 g and 20 minutes over. For joints over 10 lb/4.5 kg, allow 15 minutes per lb/450 g and 15 minutes over. Put the joint into a large pan and cover with cold water, adding flavourings such as peppercorns, cloves and root vegetables. Bring slowly to the boil and remove any scum. Cover and simmer gently, timing from when boiling point was reached. If a joint is to be used cold, leave it to cool in the cooking liquid so that it remains moist and full of flavour. Remove the skin before serving.
Cuts to use Collar; forehock; gammon hock.

ROASTING   Calculate the cooking time as for boiling. Simmer for half the cooking time, then strip off the skin and put the joint into a roasting

Derinding and stretching a bacon rasher

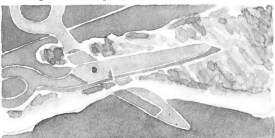

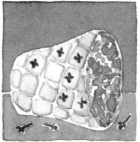

Stripping, scoring and decorating a gammon joint

tin. Roast at 180°C/350°F/Gas Mark 4 until 15 minutes before the end of cooking time, then increase oven to 220°C/425°F/Gas Mark 7 for 15 minutes, basting the joint frequently.
Cuts to use Corner gammon; forehock; gammon hock.

BAKING Calculate the cooking time as for boiling. Simmer for half the cooking time, then wrap in foil and cook at 180°C/350°F/Gas Mark 4 until 30 minutes before the end of cooking time. Strip off skin and score the fat in diamonds. Stud with cloves and sprinkle with brown sugar. Bake at 220°C/425°F/Gas Mark 7 for 30 minutes. For a more elaborate glaze involving honey, cider, *etc.*, only bake for 20 minutes when the glaze has been applied to prevent burning.
Cuts to use Corner gammon; gammon hock.

BRAISING First simmer the joint for half the cooking time, as you would before baking (see page 9). Then skin it and place in a casserole on a bed of lightly fried chopped vegetables such as carrots, and onions or leeks. Pour over about $\frac{1}{2}$ pint/300 ml of the boiling liquid – you should have just enough to give a shallow 'bath' for the bacon to cook in. Put into a moderate oven 180°C/350°F/Gas Mark 4 and finish the cooking, again allowing 20 minutes per lb/450 g and 20 minutes over. Remove the lid from the casserole for the last 30 minutes of braising, to allow the top to brown a little.
Cuts to use Collar; forehock; middle cut.

PRESSURE COOKING Take out the trivet or rack and use your pressure cooker as you would a normal saucepan. Bring the joint to a boil, then remove and drain it. Replace the trivet, place the bacon on it, and cook according to the chart for your pressure cooker. As with braising, the addition of a few simple root vegetables will give extra flavour.
Cuts to use Collar; forehock; middlecut and streaky joints.

SUCCESS FOR STARTERS
STOCK, SOUPS & APPETISERS

Not many people think of bacon or ham as a first course, but its appetising flavour and attractive appearance are perfect for setting the scene for a formal meal. A first course should be tempting and a little unusual, but should not be so heavy that it dulls the appetite for following courses.

Bacon is an important ingredient in pâtés and soups, but it also pairs well with seafood and with fruit for tempting little dishes. While all the following recipes are ideal first courses, they are so delicious that they may be served in larger portions for luncheons and suppers, followed by a light pudding, or just fruit and cheese.

Don't forget the accompaniments to these dishes which make them particularly attractive – warm fingers of toast, crisp Melba toast, or thin brown bread and butter, and perhaps a salad garnish.

BACON STOCK

Bacon stock is often used for soup. This is most simply the liquid in which a bacon joint has been cooked, and it has an excellent flavour if peppercorns, bay leaves, carrots and onions have been included in the water. The liquid should be strained and left until cold, and then surplus fat removed (this will form a layer on the surface). If the liquid is salty, boil it again with a potato which will absorb excess salt. Discard the potato before using the stock.

HAM AND GREEN PEA SOUP
SERVES 4

8 oz/225 g green split peas, soaked
1 small onion
1 small carrot
bay leaf, thyme and parsley
2 pints/1.2 l stock from cooking bacon joint
pepper
$\frac{1}{2}$ oz/15 g butter

Garnish
2 oz/50 g cooked bacon, finely diced
2 teaspoons finely chopped fresh chives or mint

Drain the soaked peas and put into a pan with the onion, carrot, herbs and stock. Bring to the boil, then cover and simmer until the peas are very soft. Remove and discard the herbs. If a smooth soup is liked, make into a purée in a blender or food processor. Reheat the soup and season to taste with pepper. Stir in the butter. Serve garnished with the finely diced bacon and chopped herbs. *Photographed on page 15*

HAM FRITTERS
SERVES 6

3 oz/75 g butter
salt
4 oz/100 g plain flour
4 eggs
1 × 5 oz/150 g slice of cooked ham
2 tablespoons walnuts, chopped
oil for deep frying

Bring 8 fl oz/250 ml water to a boil in a saucepan, together with the butter and a pinch of salt. Add the flour all at once. Mix vigorously with a wooden spoon until the dough comes away from the sides of the pan. Remove the pan from the heat. Add one egg and mix thoroughly, then add another egg and mix. Continue adding eggs, incorporating each one thoroughly before adding the next.

Cut the ham into small cubes and mix into the choux pastry, together with the chopped walnuts.

Heat oil for deep frying to 175°C/345°F.

Take a teaspoon of the pastry and drop into the oil, using another teaspoon to loosen the pastry. Continue adding balls of pastry to the oil, cooking about a dozen at a time. Cook the fritters for 5–6 minutes or until they are well browned.

Drain the fritters on a plate lined with paper towels. Serve hot, with apple sauce (see page 137), apricot sauce (see page 134), or a raisin sauce (page 138). *Photographed on page 15.*

BACON-STUFFED MUSSELS
SERVES 6

6 lb/3 kg mussels, scrubbed and cleaned
$\frac{1}{4}$ pint/150 ml dry white wine
4 oz/100 g mushrooms
4 rashers streaky bacon, cooked until crisp
about 2 oz/50 g breadcrumbs
1 tablespoon chopped parsley
salt and pepper
butter

Put the scrubbed mussels into a heavy pan and open them over heat, with the white wine. Shake the pan gently, with the lid on, for about 5 minutes until the mussels begin to open. As they do so, remove to a colander. Discard any mussels that refuse to open. Remove and discard the half shell from each one. Strain and save the cooking liquor.

To make the stuffing, chop the mushrooms finely and crumble the bacon. Mix them together with the parsley and strained mussel cooking liquor. Stir in enough breadcrumbs to make a normal stuffing consistency – workable but not wet. Season to taste. Divide this mixture between the shells, to cover the mussels. Dot with butter and bake in a moderate oven, 180°C/350°F/Gas Mark 4, until brown and bubbling. Alternatively, finish off – carefully – under a hot grill.

Ham and green pea soup (page 12), bacon-stuffed mussels,
and ham fritters (page 13) with apricot sauce (page 134)

WINTER ARTICHOKE SOUP
SERVES 4

1 lb/450 g Jerusalem artichokes, sliced
3 medium potatoes, diced
1 medium leek, thinly sliced
1 pint/600 ml bacon stock or water
1 pint/600 ml creamy milk
1 oz/25 g butter
salt and pepper
4 streaky bacon rashers
1 tablespoon chopped parsley

Put the vegetables into a pan with the bacon stock or water. Bring to the boil and then cover and simmer for about 30 minutes until the vegetables are very soft. Put through a sieve or blend into a purée. Return to the pan with the milk and simmer for 15 minutes. Stir in the butter and season with salt and pepper.

Grill the bacon until crisp and crumble into small pieces. Pour the soup into 4 bowls and sprinkle with bacon and parsley.

LEEK, BACON AND POTATO SOUP
SERVES 4

2 streaky bacon rashers, finely chopped
2 oz/50 g butter
4 medium leeks, cleaned and sliced thinly into rings
1 small onion, finely chopped
3 medium potatoes, diced
2 pints/1.2 l bacon stock or water
2 tablespoons single cream
1 tablespoon finely chopped chives

Put the bacon and butter into a pan and heat until the butter has melted. Add the leeks and onion and stir over low heat for five minutes until soft and golden. Add the potatoes and continue cooking and stirring for 3 minutes.

Add the stock or water and bring to the boil. Cover and simmer for about 45 minutes until the vegetables are soft but not broken. If a smooth soup is preferred, cook for 10 minutes longer and blend in a liquidiser. Pour into soup bowls, put a swirl of cream in each, and sprinkle with chives.

LENTIL AND BACON SOUP
SERVES 4

4 oz/100 g lentils
1 large carrot, chopped
1 large onion, chopped
3 streaky bacon rashers, chopped
$1\frac{1}{2}$ pints/900 ml bacon stock or water
$\frac{1}{2}$ pint/300 ml milk
2 teaspoons plain flour
salt and pepper

Soak the lentils in cold water for 1 hour and then drain well. Put into a pan. Add the carrot, onion and bacon to the pan with the stock or water. Bring to the boil, cover and simmer for 1 hour. Mix two tablespoons milk with the flour and add to the remaining milk. Stir into the soup and bring to the boil again. Simmer for 5 minutes and season with salt and pepper.

If a smooth soup is preferred, the lentil mixture may be blended before the milk is added. The soup is very filling and can be a complete meal if served with wholemeal or crusty bread.

BACON PÂTÉ
SERVES 8

12 oz/350 g unsmoked streaky bacon rashers
1 lb/450 g lean pork
1 small onion
6 oz/175 g day-old white bread
2 eggs
salt and pepper
pinch of ground nutmeg
pinch of mixed fresh herbs

Derind the bacon and smooth out 6 rashers with a broad-bladed knife. Line a 2 lb/900 g terrine, loaf tin or casserole with these rashers. Chop the remaining bacon, pork and onion and put through the mincer or chop very finely in a food processor. Make the bread into crumbs and mix with the meat. Add the eggs, salt, pepper, nutmeg and herbs and mix well. Put into the bacon-lined container and cover with a lid or foil.

Put the container into a roasting tin with hot water to come half-way up the dish. Cook at 180°C/350°F/Gas Mark 4 for $1\frac{1}{2}$ hours. Remove the lid and cover the pâté with foil,. Put on heavy weights and leave for 24 hours in a cold place. Turn out of the container and serve in slices with toast or salad, or in sandwiches.

CHICKEN AND BACON PÂTÉ
SERVES 4

6 oz/175 g cooked chicken, roughly chopped
4 back bacon rashers
1 small onion, roughly chopped
3 oz/75 g full fat soft cream cheese
1 tablespoon dry sherry
$\frac{1}{2}$ teaspoon mixed fresh herbs
salt and pepper

Grill the bacon until cooked but not crisp and cut into pieces. Put the chicken, bacon, onion and other ingredients into a blender and blend until smooth. Chill and serve with toast.

LIVER AND BACON PÂTÉ
SERVES 8

12 oz/350 g streaky bacon rashers
8 oz/225 g pig's liver, roughly chopped
1 large onion, roughly chopped
1 garlic clove, chopped
2 oz/50 g butter
salt and pepper
3 bay leaves

Foundation sauce

$\frac{1}{2}$ pint/300 ml milk
2 blades mace
1 bay leaf
2 peppercorns
1 oz/25 g butter
1 oz/25 g plain flour

Derind the bacon and smooth out 6 rashers with a broad-bladed knife. Line a 2 lb/900 g terrine, loaf tin or casserole with these rashers. Chop the remaining bacon roughly and cook it, with the liver, onion and garlic, in the butter over low heat for 10 minutes. Mince finely or chop finely in a food processor.

Prepare the sauce by heating the milk with the mace, bay leaf and peppercorns to boiling point. Leave to stand for 10 minutes and strain. Melt the butter and stir in the flour. Cook for 1 minute. Take off the heat and gradually stir in the milk. Return to the heat and bring to the boil, stirring all the time until the sauce thickens. Add to the liver mixture and beat well, seasoning to taste.

Put the mixture into the prepared container and top with the bay leaves. Cover with a lid or foil and place in a roasting tin with hot water to come half-way up the dish. Cook at 180°C/350°F/Gas Mark 4 for $1\frac{1}{4}$ hours. Cool under weights for 24 hours before slicing to serve with toast or salad.

PRAWNS WRAPPED IN BACON WITH CORN SALAD

SERVES 4

12 large prawns
12 rashers of bacon
oil for grilling
freshly ground black pepper

To serve
corn salad (lamb's lettuce)
lemon juice

Shell and clean the prawns and wrap in the bacon. Brush with a little oil and season with black pepper. Place under a hot grill and cook for about 4 minutes on each side.

Serve on a bed of corn salad dressed with a little lemon juice. *See frontispiece*

LITTLE HAM SOUFFLÉS

SERVES 6

8 oz/225 g lean cooked ham
1 oz/25 g butter · 1 oz/25 g plain flour
generous $\frac{1}{4}$ pint/150 ml single cream
3 eggs, separated
salt and pepper
pinch of ground nutmeg

Preheat the oven to 190°C/375°F/Gas Mark 5.

Using a food processor, process the ham finely, and season well.

Make a thick sauce with the butter, flour and cream, following the method for white sauce described on page 128, cooking it until it comes away from the sides of the pan. Add to the ham in the food processor bowl and blend together. Reheat this mixture in the saucepan, but do not allow to boil. Off the heat, add the egg yolks, one at a time.

Whisk the egg whites until they are stiff. Fold them lightly into the ham mixture and pour into 6 individual buttered soufflé dishes.

Bake in the preheated oven for about 10 minutes until well risen and golden. Serve at once.

BACON, AVOCADO AND ARTICHOKE SALAD
SERVES 4

This sophisticated salad has been specially devised by David Sherratt, head chef at The Bull in Long Melford, Suffolk.

2 oz/50 g butter
4 rashers smoked back bacon, cut into $\frac{1}{4}$ in/$\frac{1}{2}$ cm strips
2 garlic cloves, finely chopped
2 ripe avocados
4 tomatoes, peeled, deseeded and finely diced
4 artichoke hearts (fresh or canned), finely sliced
1 raddichio lettuce
1 orange, segmented and sprigs of parsley for garnish

Walnut dressing
2 teaspoons English mustard
juice of 1 lemon
pinch of caster sugar (optional)
6 fl oz/175 ml walnut oil
2 tablespoons chopped walnuts

Melt the butter in a heavy-bottomed saucepan, taking care that it does not colour. Put in the bacon and garlic and fry lightly for 2–3 minutes, stirring all the time. Remove from the heat.

Cut the avocados in half lengthwise and ease out the stones with a teaspoon; scoop out the flesh with a small melon baller. Make up the dressing: put the mustard and lemon juice, and sugar if wished, into a small bowl. Gradually whisk in the walnut oil. Stir in chopped walnuts.

Add the tomatoes and artichokes to the bacon, return to the heat and toss quickly. Cook for 2–3 minutes without browning. Add the walnut dressing and avocado and toss quickly but gently over a medium heat.

Serve right away, while still warm, on a bed of washed and dried raddichio leaves, decorated with orange segments and sprigs of parsley. *Photographed on page 23*

STILTON AND BACON PEARS
SERVES 4

8 canned pear halves
lettuce leaves or radicchio
2 oz/50 g Stilton cheese
4 oz/100 g full fat soft cream cheese
2 tablespoons double cream
2 teaspoons finely chopped chives
salt and pepper
3 back bacon rashers

Use high-quality firm pear halves and drain them well. Arrange a bed of lettuce or radicchio leaves on 4 serving plates and put two pear halves on each one. Crumble the Stilton cheese into a bowl and add the cream cheese and double cream. Beat together with a fork or wooden spoon until light and creamy. Add the chives and season well with salt and pepper. Pile into the cavities of the pears. Grill the bacon until crisp, and crumble into small pieces. Sprinkle on to the pears just before serving.

Stilton and bacon pears, bacon, avocado and artichoke salad (page 21),
and bacon mille feuilles (page 25)

SPINACH AND BACON SALAD
SERVES 4

1 lb/450 g fresh young spinach
4 back bacon rashers
4 oz/100 g button mushrooms, thinly sliced
1 hardboiled egg, finely chopped
6 tablespoons olive oil
2 tablespoons tarragon vinegar
salt and pepper
2 teaspoons chopped fresh tarragon

Wash the spinach very thoroughly. Drain and pat dry with kitchen paper. Remove and discard the stems and any discoloured leaves. Grill the bacon until crisp and crumble finely. Mix the bacon and spinach in a salad bowl. Add the mushrooms and egg.

Mix the oil, vinegar, salt, pepper and tarragon. Just before serving, pour over the salad and toss well. Serve with wholemeal rolls, or chunks of French bread.

CHICKEN LIVER AND BACON WARM SALAD
SERVES 4

8 oz/225 g chicken livers
4 back bacon rashers, finely chopped
1 small crisp lettuce or radicchio
8 radishes, thinly sliced
6 tablespoons walnut or hazelnut oil
2 tablespoons red wine vinegar
salt and pepper
1 teaspoon French mustard
2 teaspoons finely chopped chives

Cut each chicken liver into 3–4 pieces. Put into a pan with the bacon and toss over low heat until the chicken livers are cooked through but still lightly pink inside.

Arrange a bed of lettuce or radicchio leaves on each serving plate and sprinkle with radishes. Mix together the oil, vinegar and plenty of salt and pepper and add the mustard. Pile the warm livers and bacon on the salad leaves. Pour over the dressing, sprinkle with chives and serve at once, with crusty rolls.

BACON MILLE FEUILLES
SERVES 6

8 oz/225 g made puff pastry (see page 142)
2 oz/50 g butter
4 oz/100 g plain flour
$\frac{1}{2}$ pint/300 ml milk
4 eggs
8 oz/225 g cooked ham, diced
$\frac{1}{4}$ pint/150 ml double cream
a little beaten egg for glazing

Roll out the pastry and cut into diamond shapes about 3 in/7.5 cm long, or 3 in/7.5 cm squares, and leave to rest for 20 minutes.

Score half the pastry shapes diagonally across their surface if you wish – these will form the more decorative tops of the cases later. Bake them on a baking sheet in a hot oven 220°C/ 425°F/Gas Mark 7, for 10–15 minutes. Cool on a wire rack.

Melt the butter, add the flour and cook over a low heat for 4–5 minutes. Then add the milk and beat in the eggs. Stir in the ham and the double cream.

Pipe or spoon the ham mixture into half the pastry diamonds or squares – those not scored – and place the remaining halves on top. Brush with beaten egg and brown in the oven or under the grill. Serve hot. *Photographed on page 23*

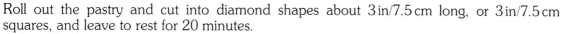

BACON-STUFFED PANCAKES WITH CHEESE SAUCE
SERVES 4

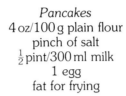

Pancakes
4 oz/100 g plain flour
pinch of salt
$\frac{1}{2}$ pint/300 ml milk
1 egg
fat for frying

Filling and topping
6 oz/175 g cooked bacon, finely chopped
1 small onion, finely chopped
4 oz/100 g button mushrooms, finely sliced
1 oz/25 g butter
$\frac{3}{4}$ pint/450 ml hot cheese sauce (page 128)
salt and pepper
1 oz/25 g grated Parmesan cheese

Prepare the pancakes first. Sieve the flour and salt into a bowl and make a well in the centre. Add the milk and egg and beat well to make a creamy batter. Grease a 7 in/17.5 cm frying pan lightly, and fry 8 thin pancakes. Keep warm on a plate over a pan of boiling water.

Put the onion and mushrooms into a pan with the butter and stir over low heat until just soft and golden. Stir in the bacon and mix well. Remove from heat and stir in $\frac{1}{4}$ pint/150 ml cheese sauce. Season to taste with salt and pepper.

Divide the mixture between the pancakes and roll them up. Arrange in a single layer in an ovenware dish. Spon over the remaining sauce and sprinkle with Parmesan cheese. Put under a hot grill until the sauce is bubbling and golden. Serve at once.

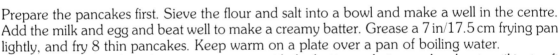

SOUR CREAM AND BACON PANCAKES WITH MELON
SERVES 4

8 pancakes (*see recipe opposite*)
8 oz/225 g streaky bacon rashers
1 melon
$\frac{1}{2}$ pint/300 ml soured cream
1 garlic clove, crushed
1 tablespoon fresh chopped dill *or* 1 teaspoon dried dill weed
salt and freshly ground black pepper
4 oz/100 g Cheddar cheese, freshly grated

Grill or fry the bacon until crisp. Drain it on absorbent kitchen paper and, when cool enough to handle, crumble it.

Halve the melon, scoop out all the seeds and scoop out the flesh with a melon ball cutter. Set aside.

In a bowl combine the bacon, soured cream, dill and garlic. Season with salt and pepper. Mix well, and divide the mixture between the pancakes. Roll them up and arrange in an ovenproof dish large enough to hold the pancakes in one layer.

Sprinkle the pancakes with grated cheese, cover with foil and place them in a preheated moderately hot oven, 190°C/375°F/Gas Mark 5 for 20 minutes.

Just before serving, garnish the pancakes with the melon balls. Serve right away.

DEVILLED KIDNEYS IN BACON
SERVES 8

8 lamb's kidneys
16 rashers (about 1 lb/450 g) streaky bacon, cut in half

For the devil mixture
1 tablespoon tomato ketchup
2 tablespoons Worcestershire sauce
2 teaspoons soy sauce
1 teaspoon sugar
$\frac{1}{2}$ teaspoon pepper
$\frac{1}{2}$ teaspoon cayenne pepper
$\frac{1}{2}$ teaspoon ground ginger
$\frac{1}{2}$ teaspoon dry mustard

4 kebab skewers

Cut the core from the kidneys with scissors or a sharp knife and cut each one into equal quarters. In a bowl, mix the ketchup, Worcestershire sauce and soy sauce, sugar, peppers, ginger and mustard. Add the kidneys and toss until well coated. Cover and leave to stand in the refrigerator for a least 3 and up to 12 hours.

A short time before serving, heat the grill. Roll each piece of kidney in a half strip of bacon and thread 4 rolls on to each kebab skewer.

Grill for 5 minutes on each side, or fry over fairly high heat until the bacon is browned.

POTTED BACON
SERVES 6

This is a practical and delicious way of making the most of the end of a large bacon joint. It will keep well for up to a week in the refrigerator.

5 oz/150 g butter
12 oz/350 g lean cooked bacon
2 tablespoons fresh chopped parsley
2 teaspoons Dijon mustard
2 tablespoons Madeira or dry sherry
good pinch of ground nutmeg
about 4 tablespoons stock or cream
freshly ground black pepper
6 small fresh bay leaves for garnish

Melt the butter in a small saucepan over a gentle heat. Mince the bacon, with 4 tablespoons of the butter, in a food processor. Cook the rest of the butter, without stirring, until it begins to foam, then remove from the heat and leave to stand.

Add the remaining ingredients to the bacon mixture, incorporating enough stock or cream to achieve a smooth paste. Put into 6 small soufflé dishes or ramekins, pressing down the contents well and smoothing the surface.

When you can see that the milky content of the butter has sunk to the bottom, leaving a clear yellow liquid, pour this liquid carefully through muslin into a jug, and then pour this clarifed butter over the potted bacon. Leave to cool, then garnish each one with a bay leaf. Serve with hot toast and butter.

BAKED BACON AND AVOCADO CHAUCER
SERVES 4

Bacon and avocado make original partners, and appear to great effect here in this recipe created by Martin Wickham, head chef at The Chaucer in Canterbury.

2 ripe avocados
4 rashers back bacon
$\frac{1}{2}$ oz/15 g clarified butter (see page 29)
2 tablespoons white wine
$\frac{1}{4}$ pint/150 ml cream
freshly ground black pepper
2 oz/50 g grated cheese
sprigs of parsley for garnish

Skin and remove the stones from the 2 avocados, and dice the flesh into $\frac{1}{4}$ in/$\frac{1}{2}$ cm cubes. Cut the bacon into strips.

Melt the clarified butter in a pan. Put in the avocado and bacon and toss gently over a moderate heat until the bacon is cooked. Moisten with the white wine, stir over the heat for a few minutes to reduce it, then add the cream. Bring briefly to a boil, then divide the mixture between 4 avocado dishes or other appropriate dishes.

Season with freshly ground black pepper and sprinkle the grated cheese over the top. Bake in a moderate oven, 180°C/350°F/Gas Mark 4 for 10 minutes. Serve hot, garnished with parsley sprigs.

READY, STEADY, GO
FAST SUPPERS AND SNACKS,
BRUNCHES & BREAKFASTS

What can be better than bacon to provide a speedy meal which is so often needed in busy households? Every wise cook keeps a pack of bacon in the refrigerator for those solitary snacks, for the unexpected hordes of teenagers, the casual visitor, or the informal supper when nobody feels like serious cooking.

Bacon is full of flavour and quick to cook, and it also pairs well with other items in the store cupboard such as cheese, eggs, bread and pasta, frozen vegetables and canned fruit. Bacon can also give a lift to those oddments like cooked vegetables, leftover potatoes and bits of cooked chicken, and transform them into a delicious but speedy dish.

CROQUE MONSIEUR
SERVES 1

2 thin slices white bread
$\frac{1}{2}$ oz/15 g softened butter
2 thin slices Gruyère or Edam cheese
1 slice cooked ham, trimmed to fit the shape and size of the bread slice
a little oil for frying

Lay one slice of bread on a bread board or work surface and spread it with a little butter. Cover with a slice of cheese, the slice of ham, then the second slice of cheese. Spread the second slice of bread with butter and lay it face down on top. Press down well to 'set' the sandwich, and trim off the crusts.

Melt the rest of the butter, with a very little oil, in a frying pan and brown the sandwiches slowly. Allow 3 minutes or so each side so that the cheese has time to melt.

Croque monsieur is an excellent idea for a sandwich toaster. In that case, don't forget to spread the butter on the *outside* of the slices of bread.

BACON FRAÎZE
SERVES 4

8 eggs
3 tablespoons single cream
1 oz/25 g plain flour
8 oz/225 g streaky bacon rashers

Beat the eggs and cream with the flour to make a thin batter. Grill the bacon until just crisp. Grease a frying pan lightly and pour in half the batter. When the top has just set, arrange the bacon rashers on top. Pour on the remaining batter and cook until set. Turn carefully to brown the other side. Serve at once with mustard.

Croque monsieur, bacon fraize, and mushroom and bacon pot (page 35)

BACON TURNOVERS
SERVES 4

4 streaky bacon rashers, finely chopped
4 oz/100 g self-raising flour
1 teaspoon mixed fresh herbs
$\frac{1}{2}$ teaspoon salt
5 tablespoons milk

Put the bacon into a thick pan and heat gently until the fat runs and the bacon is just cooked through. Lift out the bacon with a slotted spoon and keep the fat in the pan. Mix the flour, herbs, salt and milk to make a soft firm dough. Roll out $\frac{1}{4}$in/$\frac{1}{2}$cm thick and cut into eight 3 in/7.5 cm rounds. Put bacon in the centre of four rounds and top with the remaining rounds, pressing them firmly togehter. Fry in the bacon fat for about 5 minutes on each side until cooked through and golden brown. Serve with tomatoes and mushrooms, or with eggs.

Note If there is not much bacon fat, add a little oil to the pan for frying.

COUNTRY OMELETTE
SERVES 1

2 streaky bacon rashers, finely chopped
1 medium potato, cut into small dice
salt and pepper
2 eggs
2 teaspoons water
1 oz/25 g butter

Put the bacon into a thick frying pan and heat gently until the fat starts to run. Add the potato to the pan and continue cooking, stirring often, until the potato is cooked. Season to taste.

Beat the eggs lightly with the water. Add the butter to the frying pan and heat until it bubbles. Pour in the eggs and stir and lift with a fork as they set. When just set, slip the omelette on to a plate without folding. Serve with grilled tomatoes or a green salad.

MUSHROOM AND BACON POT
SERVES 4

This is a light but filling bacon and mushroom snack, devised by Pat McSorley, head chef of the Rusacks Marine Hotel in Fife. Easily prepared in a few minutes, it is particularly good when served with crisp fresh French bread.

8 oz/225 g smoked back or streaky bacon rashers, cut into 1 in/2.5 cm strips
1 lb/450 g button mushrooms, sliced
4 oz/100 g onion, finely sliced
2 tablespoons butter
8 fl oz/250 ml double cream
salt and pepper
1 oz/25 g chopped parsley

Toss the bacon, mushrooms and onion together in the butter. When cooked, add the cream and simmer together for 2–3 minutes until it thickens to a good consistency. Season to taste and serve, in soup plates, sprinkled with the chopped parsley and accompanied by a stick of hot French bread. *Photographed on page 33*

BACON PAN HASH
SERVES 4

12 oz/350 g cooked bacon
1 oz/25 g butter
1 medium onion, finely chopped
2 tablespoons tomato ketchup
1 teaspoon made mustard
2 tablespoons milk
salt and pepper
1 lb/450 g cooked mashed potatoes
4 tablespoons oil

Mince the bacon, or chop finely in a food processor. Melt the butter and cook the onion over low heat for 5 minutes until soft and golden. Stir in the tomato ketchup, mustard and milk. Add the minced bacon and season well with salt and pepper.

Stir the bacon mixture into the potatoes until evenly mixed. Heat the oil in a deep frying pan. Put in the potato mixture and press down lightly. Cook over low heat until the underside is crisp and golden. Cut into wedges in the pan and serve at once with a green salad.

BACONBURGERS
SERVES 4

8 oz/225 g cooked bacon
8 oz/225 g pork sausagemeat
1 small onion, finely chopped
pinch of mixed fresh herbs
1 egg yolk
oil for frying

Mince the bacon and mix with the sausagemeat until evenly coloured. Add the onion to the meat with the herbs, egg yolk, and salt and pepper if necessary. Mix very well and divide into 8 portions.

Form the meat into flat burger shapes. Fry in hot oil for 6–7 minutes until well-browned on both sides. Serve in hot baps with tomato sauce, or with baked beans, vegetables or salad.

BACON AND KIDNEY KEBABS
SERVES 4

12 streaky bacon rashers
6 lamb's kidneys
8 mushrooms
4 tomatoes
oil
salt and pepper

Derind the bacon and cut each rasher in half. Spread thinly with a broad-bladed knife and roll up each piece of rasher. Skin the kidneys and remove the cores. Cut each kidney in half. Wipe the mushrooms and tomatoes. Thread bacon rolls, kidney halves and mushrooms on 4 kebab skewers and put a tomato on the end of each one. Brush with oil and season with salt and pepper. Grill on a cool area of the barbecue grill, or under a medium grill for 10–15 minutes, turning often. Serve with French bread and plenty of mustard.

BACON FLODDIES
SERVES 4

1 large potato
1 medium onion
1 egg
1 oz/25 g self-raising flour
4 oz/100 g back bacon rashers, derinded and finely chopped
$\frac{1}{2}$ teaspoon chopped mixed fresh herbs
salt and pepper
lard for frying

Grate the potato and onion into a bowl. Beat the egg and add to the vegetables with the flour. Add the bacon to the mixture with the herbs, and season to taste. Mix well and fry in spoonfuls in hot lard until golden on both sides and cooked through. Serve with poached or fried eggs.

BARBECUED BACON
SERVES 4

4 gammon rashers
$\frac{1}{4}$ pint/150 ml bottled savoury sauce
$1\frac{1}{2}$ tablespoons light soft brown sugar
1 tablespoon French mustard
1 tablespoon Worcestershire sauce
1 tablespoon lemon juice
3 drops Tabasco sauce

Cut the edges of the gammon rashers to prevent curling. Mix together all the other ingredients and put half into a shallow dish. Put in the rashers and cover with the remaining sauce. Leave to stand for 1 hour. Grill the rashers for 5 minutes on each side, on the barbecue or under the grill, brushing occasionally with the sauce.

BARBECUED ORANGE HAM
SERVES 4

$1\frac{1}{2}$ lb/675 g cooked ham
4 tablespoons orange juice
4 tablespoons medium sherry
$\frac{1}{2}$ teaspoon mustard powder
pinch of mixed fresh herbs
4 canned pineapple rings

Cut the ham into 1 in/2.5 cm slices. Mix together the orange juice, sherry, mustard and herbs and brush over the ham. Grill on each side on the barbecue or under the grill, brushing often with the liquid, until the slices are golden brown and piping hot. Just before cooking finishes, grill the pineapple slices for 2 minutes, basting often with the sauce. Serve the ham garnished with the pineapple slices.

FAST SUPPERS & SNACKS, BRUNCHES & BREAKFASTS

HAM FLORENTINE
SERVES 4

2 lb/1 kg fresh spinach, *or* approx 1¼ lb/550 g frozen leaf spinach
1 oz/25 g butter for greasing
4 slices cooked ham
about ½ pint/300 ml cheese sauce (*see page 128*)
grated Parmesan cheese

First, cook, drain and chop the spinach (for cooking instructions, see the first part of the recipe for creamed spinach on page 122).

Butter generously an ovenproof gratin dish, and make in it a good thick bed of cooked chopped spinach. Roll up loosely the slices of ham and arrange them on top.

Pour over the cheese sauce, sprinkle with grated Parmesan and bake the dish in a hot oven, 220°C/425°F/Gas Mark 7, for 10 minutes, until bubbling and nicely browned on top.

BACON SANDWICH
SERVES 1

2 slices white or wholemeal bread
butter for spreading
1 tablespoon chutney
2 back bacon rashers

Spread the bread with butter and then with chutney. Grill the bacon until just crisp. Cut each rasher in half. Sandwich the bread slices together with bacon. Cut into four and serve at once.

Note The sandwich may be varied by adding crisp lettuce leaves and tomato slices with a little mayonnaise; or by adding a fried egg to the bacon.

BUTTERED EGGS WITH CRISPY BACON
SERVES 4–5

8 eggs
salt and pepper
$1\frac{1}{2}$–2 oz/40–50 g softened butter
2 oz/50 g lean bacon rashers, grilled

Beat the eggs in a bowl with the seasoning until blended.

Melt half the butter in a saucepan – non-stick preferably – pour in the eggs and place over a moderate heat. Stirring continually, making sure that your wooden spoon or spatula reaches all over the base of the pan, cook gently until the eggs thicken. As soon as they have reached the right creamy consistency (they should just hold their shape in the spoon) remove from the heat. Beat in the rest of the butter; this will both enrich the dish and stop the cooking.

To serve, place on hot toast and crumble the hot grilled bacon over.

HAM AND EGG COCOTTES
SERVES 4

$\frac{1}{2}$ oz/15 g butter
2 teaspoons finely chopped parsley
2 oz/50 g cooked ham, finely chopped
4 eggs
salt and freshly ground black pepper

Grease 4 little cocotte dishes with the butter. Sprinkle each with parsley and divide the chopped ham among them.

Break an egg into each cocotte dish and season with salt and pepper. Place in a baking dish, to which you have added enough hot water to come half-way up their sides, and cook in a moderate oven, 180°C/350°F/Gas Mark 4 until the whites are set and the yolks creamy.

Buttered eggs with crispy bacon, ham and egg cocottes,
and best brunch rolls (overleaf)

BEST BRUNCH ROLLS
SERVES 4

6 rashers back bacon
4 large bread rolls
a little oil for frying
6 oz/175 g mushrooms, thinly sliced
3 oz/75 g grated Cheddar cheese
salt and pepper

Grill the bacon until crisp, then crumble.

Cut the tops off the rolls, scoop out the crumb and fry this in the bacon fat until golden.

Add a little extra oil to the pan and fry the mushrooms for 5 minutes. Mix the mushrooms and crumbs with the crumbled bacon and the grated cheese. Season. Fill the rolls with this mixture and put under a hot grill until browned. *Photographed on page 41*

CUMBERLAND BACON AND EGG PIE
SERVES 4

6 oz/175 g made shortcrust pastry (see page 142)
4 oz/100 g streaky bacon
4 eggs
seasoning
a little beaten egg to glaze

Divide the pastry into two and roll out half to line a 7 in/18 cm flat ovenproof plate. Cut up the bacon into pieces $2\frac{1}{2}$ in/6 cm long and place on the pastry, leaving 4 depressions. Break an egg into each depression and season.

Roll out the other half of the pastry, moisten the edges and cover the pie. Press the edges together and trim; decorate, using the pastry trimmings. Brush with beaten egg.

Bake in a hot oven, 220°C/425°F/Gas Mark 7, for 30 minutes.

SUNDAY OMELETTE
SERVES 2

1 chicken liver, cut into small pieces
2 streaky bacon rashers, finely chopped
1 small onion, finely chopped
2 oz/50 g button mushrooms, chopped
3 eggs
salt and pepper
1 oz/25 g butter

Put the bacon into an omelette pan. Heat until the fat runs out and the bacon begins to get crisp. Add the liver and onion and stir together for 2 minutes over low heat. Add the mushrooms to the pan, and continue stirring together for 2 minutes.

Beat the eggs lightly together and season with salt and pepper. Add the butter to the pan and leave until melted. Add the eggs and stir lightly with a fork, lifting the mixture from time to time so that liquid eggs run underneath. When the mixture has just set, divide into two pieces and lift on to hot plates without folding. Serve with crusty bread and a green salad.

BACON-AND-EGGS
SERVES 2

Melt a small nut of butter in a frying pan – non-stick preferably – over a moderate-to-low heat and place in it, close together, 4 very thin bacon rashers. Cook for just a couple of minutes until the fat is translucent, then break 2 eggs over them. Season, discreetly, with salt and pepper, turn up the heat and fry until the egg whites are cooked.

Slide on to a warmed serving dish and serve right away with toast.

HAM AND EGGS FOR 2 Make exactly as above, but use 2 slices of cooked ham instead of the bacon.

BACON RISOTTO
SERVES 4

6 oz/175 g streaky bacon
$\frac{1}{2}$ oz/15 g butter
1 tablespoon oil
1 large onion, chopped
8 oz/225 g long grain rice
4 oz/100 g shelled peas, fresh or frozen
1 pint/600 ml chicken stock

Trim the bacon and cut it into small pieces. Heat the butter and oil in a large frying pan, add the bacon and onion and fry gently for 3 minutes.

Add the rice and continue frying, stirring occasionally, for 5 minutes. Add the peas and one-third of the stock; simmer for 5 minutes, then add the remainder of the stock. Cover with a lid or foil and simmer until the rice is cooked and the stock absorbed, about 15 minutes.

Taste and correct the seasoning if necesary. Serve immediately, with a green salad.

HAM SOUFFLÉ
SERVES 4

This excellent ham soufflé is served at The Black Swan Hotel's restaurant in Helmsley according to head chef John Benson-Smith's own recipe.

2 tablespoons unsalted butter, plus a little more for greasing
2 tablespoons plain flour · $\frac{1}{2}$ pint/300 ml milk
2 oz/50 g grated Gruyère cheese
4 oz/100 g ham, finely minced
4 eggs, separated
cayenne pepper

Melt the butter in a pan and add in the flour, stirring continuously. When blended, add the cream a little at a time. Simmer for a few minutes until the sauce is thick and smooth. Leave to cool, then mix in the cheese, ham and egg yolks, well beaten. Season to taste with cayenne.

Beat the egg whites until very stiff and fold into the mixture. Turn into a buttered soufflé mould and bake in a moderate oven, 180°C/350°F/Gas Mark 4, for 25–30 minutes until well risen and golden brown. Serve immediately with cucumber relish.

BACON SCOTCH EGGS
SERVES 3–4

10 oz/300 g cooked bacon
6 eggs
salt and pepper

Grease 6 deep tartlet tins. Mince the bacon finely and pack into the bottom and sides of each tin, pressing the meat firmly. Break an egg into each tin and season with salt and pepper. Cover with foil and bake at 200°C/400°F/Gas Mark 6 for 20 minutes. Serve with vegetables or hot baps, or serve cold with salad.

DEVILLED BACON GRIDDLECAKES
SERVES 4

4 back bacon rashers
4 oz/100 g self-raising flour
1 teaspoon baking powder
$\frac{1}{2}$ teaspoon salt
1 egg
2 tablespoons salad oil
$\frac{1}{4}$ pint/150 ml milk
1 teaspoon Worcestershire sauce
oil for shallow frying

Grill the bacon until cooked through and chop roughly. Sieve the flour, baking powder and salt together and make a well in the centre. Beat the egg with the oil and milk and the sauce, and gradually add to the flour, beating well until thoroughly mixed.

Heat a large frying pan and add just enough oil to cover the base. Put tablespoons of batter in the pan, well apart, and sprinkle with pieces of bacon. Cook over low heat until the tops of the griddle cakes bubble, and they are golden brown underneath. Turn and continue cooking until golden brown on the other side. Serve at once with fried or scrambled eggs, tomatoes or sausages.

SPAGHETTI ALLA CARBONARA
SERVES 4

2 tablespoons olive or vegetable oil
3 garlic cloves, crushed and peeled
8 oz/225 g lean smoked bacon, cut into narrow strips
12 oz/350 g spaghetti
3 eggs
3 oz/75 g grated Parmesan cheese
salt and freshly ground black pepper

Heat the oil in a pan and fry the garlic in it until it is golden in colour, then remove and discard the garlic. Add the bacon to the oil in the pan and cook until it is just crisp. Set aside.

While the pasta is cooking, warm a serving bowl in a low oven. Then mix together in it the eggs and grated Parmesan cheese and season well with salt and pepper.

When the pasta is cooked 'al dente', drain it and toss it in the serving bowl with the egg and cheese mixture. Reheat the bacon and add it also, together with its fat, to the pasta. Toss all together thoroughly so that the heat from the spaghetti cooks the eggs and they coat the pasta.

Serve right away, with a green salad.

BARBECUED SCALLOPS AND BACON
SERVES 4

24 small scallops
8 oz/225 g streaky bacon rashers
oil
salt and pepper · few drops of Tabasco sauce

Cut the rashers in half and flatten each half with a broad-bladed knife. Wrap each scallop in a piece of bacon and thread 6 scallops on each of 4 skewers. Season the oil with salt, pepper and Tabasco sauce, and brush over the scallops. Cook over a hot barbecue, or under a hot grill, brushing with oil frequently. Serve with wedges of lemon and Tartare sauce.

Barbecued scallops and bacon, spaghetti alla carbonara,
and quiche Lorraine (overleaf)

QUICHE LORRAINE
SERVES 4–6

12 oz/350 g made shortcrust pastry (see page 142)
7 oz/200 g lean bacon, either diced (if it is from a piece) or cut into thin strips
3 eggs
$\frac{1}{2}$ pint/300 ml single cream
salt and pepper
grated nutmeg
$\frac{1}{2}$ oz/15 g butter

Roll out the pastry and use it to line an 8-in/20-cm flan or pie tin. Place this on a baking sheet and bake blind in a moderately hot oven, 200°C/400°F/Gas Mark 6, for about 15 minutes or until the pastry is beginning to colour and to shrink away from the sides of the tin or dish.

Meanwhile, prepare the filling. Fry the bacon in a non-stick frying pan until it is brown and place it in the baked pastry shell.

Beat the eggs, cream and seasonings together in a bowl until blended. Check the seasoning, and pour into the pastry shell. Cut the butter into small pieces and scatter over the top.

Return the quiche to the oven and bake it for 25–30 minutes, or until the quiche has puffed up, is set and golden brown. Serve warm. *Photographed on page 47*

HAM AND HADDIE
SERVES 6

This modern version of a traditional Scottish favourite comes from Colin Chalmers, head chef at the Atholl Palace Hotel in Pitlochry, Perthshire.

12 oz/350 g yellow smoked haddock fillets
$\frac{1}{2}$ pint/300 ml milk
2 oz/50 g butter, plus a little extra for greasing
2 oz/50 g plain flour
4 oz/100 g grated Cheddar or Swiss cheese
$\frac{1}{4}$ pint/150 ml single cream
12 oz/350 g cooked ham slices

Place the haddock fillets in a heavy saucepan, pour over the milk and bring to a boil. Keeping the liquid at a very gentle simmer, poach the fish for 5 minutes. Drain, then flake it, reserving the poaching milk.

Melt the butter in a small saucepan, add the flour and cook over a low heat for 2 minutes. Whisk in the reserved hot milk, bring the sauce to a boil, lower the heat and simmer gently for 5 minutes. Stir in the grated cheese and the cream and season to taste. You will have a heavy sauce; use a little of it to bind the flaked fish by mixing them lightly together.

Lay the slices of cooked ham flat, divide the smoked haddock mixture among them, roll them up and place in a greased shallow ovenproof dish, in one layer. Pour over the remaining cheese sauce and put into a hot oven, 210°C/425°F/Gas Mark 7, or under a grill to heat through and brown on top. *Photographed on page 75*

NORFOLK BACON, CHICKEN AND MUSHROOM SKILLET
SERVES 4

Devised by George Price, head chef at The Bell Hotel in Thetford, Norfolk, this recipe just needs toast fingers and perhaps a side salad as well to make the perfect supper.

3 oz/75 g butter
4 oz/100 g back bacon, chopped
3 oz/75 g cooked white chicken meat, diced
3 oz/75 g button mushrooms, quartered

White sauce

2 oz/50 g butter
2 oz/50 g plain flour
$\frac{1}{2}$ pint/300 ml hot milk
salt and pepper
3 tablespoons grated Gruyère or Cheddar cheese

Melt the butter in a frying pan. Add the bacon, chicken and mushrooms and cook gently, stirring occasionally, for 8–10 minutes.

Meanwhile, make the sauce. Put the butter into a small saucepan and melt it over a gentle heat. Add the flour, mix it in well and cook together for 1 minute. Add the hot milk slowly and cook over a low heat, stirring with a wooden spoon, until all the butter and flour mixture has been absorbed and the white sauce is rich and creamy.

Add the bacon mixture to the white sauce and stir together for a few minutes to heat through. Season to taste. Divide among 4 fireproof dishes. Sprinkle grated cheese on top and brown under the grill.

Serve hot, accompanied by toast fingers.

MAIN ATTRACTIONS
REGIONAL DISHES, PARTY PIECES
& BUFFETS

For centuries, bacon and ham have been the centre of popular meals all over Europe. In the olden days, meat had to be salted for winter storage, and everyone found that pork responded best of all to the salting process, yielding a tender pink meat which was full of flavour. Many traditional pies, puddings and casseroles have been based on bacon, but this delicious meat has also been translated into the more sophisticated dishes which make use of the fine leg joint known as ham. Large joints and gammon steaks are ideal for entertaining, and there is no waste as cooked ham can be transformed into many delicious dishes (*if* there are any leftovers).

ABERDEEN ROLL
SERVES 6–8

2 lb/900 g chuck steak
12 oz/350 g back bacon rashers
1 small onion
4 oz/100 g porridge oats
1 tablespoon Worcestershire sauce
1 egg, beaten
1 teaspoon mixed fresh herbs
salt and pepper

Cut the steak, bacon and onion into pieces and mince finely. Work in the oats, sauce, egg, herbs, salt and pepper. Shape into a long thick sausage and wrap in foil. Put on a baking sheet and bake at 160°C/325°F/Gas Mark 3 for 2 hours. Unwrap and leave to cool. Serve cold in thick slices with salad.

NORTHUMBERLAND BACON CAKE
SERVES 4–6

1 lb/450 g plain flour
1 teaspoon baking powder
8 oz/225 g lard
8 oz/225 g cold boiled bacon, thinly sliced

Sieve the flour and baking powder into a bowl. Rub in the lard until the mixture is like fine breadcrumbs. Add just enough cold water to make a firm pastry. Roll the pastry into a 10 in/ 25 cm circle. Cover half the pastry completely with bacon slices. Fold over the other half of the pastry and roll it gently to drive out the air. Prick all over with a fork and pinch the edges together firmly. Put on to a baking sheet and bake at 190°C/375°F/Gas Mark 5 for 45 minutes. Eat freshly baked, either hot or cold.

HUNTINGDON FIDGET PIE
SERVES 4

1 lb/450 g potatoes, thinly sliced
1 lb/450 g dessert apples, peeled and thinly sliced
8 oz/225 g streaky bacon rashers, chopped
salt and pepper
$\frac{1}{2}$ pint/300 ml stock
8 oz/225 g made shortcrust pastry

Arrange the potatoes, apples and bacon in layers in a pie dish, seasoning the layers well with salt and pepper. Pour in the stock. Cover with the pastry and make a small slit in the top. Bake at 200°C/400°F/Gas Mark 6 for 30 minutes, then at 180°C/350°F/Gas Mark 4 for 30 minutes, covering the pastry with a double sheet of greaseproof paper if it becomes too brown.

WELSH MISER'S FEAST
SERVES 4

1 lb/450 g potatoes, thickly sliced
8 oz/225 g onions, thinly sliced
8 oz/225 g streaky bacon rashers, chopped
salt and pepper
$\frac{1}{2}$ pint/300 ml water

Arrange potatoes, onions and bacon in alternating layers in a casserole, finishing with a layer of potatoes. Season each layer with salt and pepper. Pour in the water, cover and cook at 160°C/325°F/Gas Mark 3 for 2 hours. Remove lid and continue cooking for 20 minutes. It was said that a miser would eat the potatoes one day and enjoy the bacon on a second day.

LINCOLNSHIRE CHINE
SERVES 4–6

The traditional 'chine' is a chunky piece of bacon running down from the neck which gives a good proportion of lean and fat. The joint is stuffed with a large quantity of fresh herbs, including raspberry leaves, and when it is cut shows a lovely pattern of pink and green stripes. The following recipe gives a simple everyday version to make with a small bacon joint.

3 lb/1.35 kg gammon or forehock joint · 6 tablespoons chopped mixed fresh herbs

With a very sharp knife, cut down through the bacon joint in 4–5 places, just leaving the base uncut. Stuff the herbs between the slices and tie the joint two or three times very firmly. Tie the joint in a piece of muslin to hold the herbs. Put into a pan and cover with fresh cold water. Bring to the boil, then cover and simmer for $1\frac{1}{4}$ hours. Cool in the cooking liquid. Drain and put on to a board. Remove the strings and skin, and press the joint under weights until completely cold. Cut in thick slices to show the stripes, and serve with pickles or salad.

NORTHAMPTONSHIRE BACON ROLL
SERVES 4

6 oz/175 g streaky bacon rashers, finely chopped
8 oz/225 g self-raising flour · 3 oz/75 g shredded suet
salt and pepper · 1 medium onion, finely chopped

Prepare the pastry by stirring together flour, suet and a pinch of salt until evenly mixed. Add just enough cold water to make a firm dough. Roll out on a floured board into a rectangle about 8×12 in/20 × 30 cm.

Mix the bacon and onion and season well with salt and pepper. Arrange on the pastry and roll up like a Swiss roll. Tie into a floured cloth and place in a pan of boiling water. Boil for $1\frac{1}{2}$ hours. Unroll carefully on a serving dish, and serve with gravy and vegetables.

Two regional classics from the Midlands, Northamptonshire bacon roll
and Lincolnshire chine, served with pickles

WEST COUNTRY BACON WITH OATCAKES
SERVES 4–6

4 oz/100 g medium oatmeal
$\frac{1}{2}$ pint/300 ml milk
3 oz/75 g shredded suet
1 oz/25 g plain flour
salt and pepper
8 back bacon rashers
1 oz/25 g lard

Soak the oatmeal in the milk until the liquid has been absorbed. Mix in the suet and flour and season well with salt and pepper. Place the mixture on a floured board and shape into small round flat cakes.

Fry the bacon in the lard until cooked. Lift out the bacon, drain well and keep hot. Fry the oatcakes in the fat, cooking them on both sides until golden brown and cooked through. Serve hot with the bacon.

NORFOLK PLOUGH PUDDING
SERVES 6

12 oz/350 g self-raising flour
6 oz/175 g shredded suet
salt and pepper
1 lb/450 g pork sausagemeat
6 oz/175 g streaky bacon rashers, finely chopped
1 medium onion, finely chopped
2 teaspoons sage
4 tablespoons stock or water

Stir together the flour, suet and a pinch of salt until evenly mixed. Add enough cold water to make a firm dough. Line a 2 pint/1.2 l pudding basin with two-thirds of the pastry. Press the sausagemeat round the pastry lining the bowl, leaving a hole in the centre. Mix the bacon, onion and sage and season well with salt and pepper. Place in the hole and sprinkle with stock or water. Cover with the remaining pastry.

Cover with greaseproof paper and foil and tie firmly. Put into a pan with boiling water to come half-way up the basin. Cover and simmer for 2 hours, adding more boiling water to the pan from time to time. Turn out and serve with gravy and vegetables.

SUSSEX BACON PUDDING
SERVES 6

8 oz/225 g self-raising flour
3 oz/75 g shredded suet
6 oz/175 g streaky bacon rashers, finely chopped
1 medium onion, finely chopped
1 tablespoon chopped mixed fresh herbs
1 egg, beaten
milk
salt and pepper

Stir together the flour and suet until evenly mixed. Add the bacon, onion and herbs and again stir until evenly mixed. Add the egg and enough milk to make a firm but soft dough. Season well with salt and pepper.

Put the mixture into a well-greased pudding basin and cover with greaseproof paper and foil. Tie firmly and place in a pan of boiling water to come half-way up the bowl. Cover and simmer for 2 hours, adding more boiling water to the pan from time to time. Turn out and serve with gravy and vegetables.

IRISH BACON IN STOUT
SERVES 10–12

5 lb/2.25 kg corner gammon joint
2 pints/1.2 l Guinness
$\frac{1}{2}$ pint/300 ml water
1 small onion
1 small carrot
2 bay leaves
10 peppercorns
2 cloves

Put the gammon joint into a large pan. Pour on the Guinness and water. Add the whole onion and carrot with bay leaves, peppercorns and cloves. Bring to the boil, then cover and simmer very gently, allowing 20 minutes per lb/450 g and 20 minutes over. Leave to cool in the liquid. Drain and strip off the skin. If liked, coat the fat with dried breadcrumbs. Serve with baked jacket potatoes and vegetables, or with salad or pickles.

DUBLIN CODDLE
SERVES 4

1 lb/450 g pork sausages
2 medium onions, sliced
4 back bacon rashers, chopped
1 lb/450 g potatoes
salt and pepper
$\frac{3}{4}$ pint/450 ml stock

Prick the sausages lightly and put into a flameproof casserole in a single layer. Add the onions and bacon. Peel the potatoes and leave whole if they are medium-sized, or cut into large pieces. Add to the casserole, season well, and add the stock. Cover and simmer for $1\frac{1}{4}$ hours. Serve with wholemeal bread.

HEREFORD COBBED BACON
SERVES 4

4 gammon steaks
$\frac{1}{2}$ oz/15 g plain flour
pepper
pinch of sugar
1 oz/25 g bacon fat
2 dessert apples, peeled and quartered

Mix the flour, pepper and sugar together and lightly coat the gammon steaks. Melt the bacon fat in a shallow pan and put in the gammon steaks. Cover tightly with a lid or piece of foil and cook for 10 minutes over low heat. Turn the gammon steaks, cover and continue cooking for 10 minutes.

Cut each apple quarter in half and tuck the pieces under the gammon steaks. Cover and continue cooking for 10 minutes.

This is a very old farming dish, and was traditionally served with cabbage in parsley sauce.

KENTISH BACON AND CHERRY PIE
SERVES 4

12 oz/350 g made puff pastry
12 oz/350 g cold boiled bacon, finely chopped or minced
4 oz/100 g cherries, stoned and quartered
$\frac{1}{4}$ pint/150 ml white sauce (see page 128)
1 teaspoon mint jelly
pepper
beaten egg for glazing

Line an 8–9 in/20–22.5 cm pie plate with half the pastry. Mix the bacon and cherries into the sauce with the mint jelly and pepper. Fill the pastry case and cover with the remaining pastry, making a small hole in the lid. Glaze the pastry with the beaten egg. Bake at 220°C/425°F/Gas Mark 7 for 15 minutes, then at 190°C/375°F/Gas Mark 5 for 20 minutes. Serve hot or cold. *Photographed on page 61*

ESSEX BOILED BACON
WITH BROAD BEANS
SERVES 4–6

2 lb/900 g forehock or gammon joint
1 small onion
1 small carrot
1 bay leaf
$\frac{1}{2}$ teaspoon brown sugar
2 cloves
$1\frac{1}{2}$ lb/675 g shelled broad beans
parsley sauce (see page 128)

Put the bacon into a pan and add the whole onion and carrot, bay leaf, sugar and cloves. Just cover with water. Bring to the boil, then cover and simmer for 1 hour.

Just before the bacon is cooked, cook the beans in salted water until tender and drain well. Lift the bacon from the cooking liquid and strip off the skin. Slice thickly and arrange on a serving dish. Arrange the beans around the bacon. Serve the parsley sauce separately.

FARMHOUSE FLAN
SERVES 4–6

12 oz/350 g made shortcrust pastry (see page 142)
6 oz/175 g cooked ham, minced
4 oz/100 g cottage cheese
3 eggs, beaten
$\frac{1}{4}$ pint/150 ml soured cream
salt and pepper

Line an 8 in/20 cm flan tin with the pastry and bake blind at 200°C/400°F/Gas Mark 6 for 10 minutes. Stir together the ham and cottage cheese and add the beaten eggs and cream. Season well with salt and pepper and beat well. Pour into the pastry case and bake at 190°C/375°F/Gas Mark 5 for 30 minutes. Serve warm with salad.

Two traditional favourites from the southern counties, Essex boiled bacon with broad beans, served with parsley sauce (page 128), and Kentish bacon and cherry pie (page 59)

VEAL AND HAM PIE
SERVES 6–8

12 oz/350 g made shortcrust pastry (see page 142)
1 lb/450 g pie veal, diced
4 oz/100 g back bacon rashers, cut in strips
2 teaspoons lemon juice
pinch of fresh thyme
$\frac{1}{4}$ pint/150 ml stock or water
salt and pepper
1 hardboiled egg
beaten egg for glazing

Mix the veal and bacon and season with lemon juice and thyme. Put into a 9 in/22.5 cm pie plate with the stock or water and season well with salt and pepper. Cut the egg into eight sections and arrange on the meat, white sides uppermost.

Cover with pastry and make a hole in the centre. Brush well with beaten egg to glaze. Arrange pastry leaves around the centre hole and brush with egg. Bake at 190°C/375°F/Gas Mark 5 for 30 minutes, then at 180°C/350°F/Gas Mark 4 for 30 minutes. Serve hot or cold.

CHICKEN AND HAM PIE
SERVES 6

1 lb/450 g cooked chicken, diced
8 oz/225 g cooked ham, diced
8 oz/225 g potatoes, cubed
$\frac{1}{2}$ pint/300 ml chicken stock
$\frac{1}{2}$ pint/300 ml creamy milk
1 tablespoon chopped parsley
salt and pepper
12 oz/350 g made puff pastry (see page 142)

Mix the chicken, ham and potatoes and put into a pie dish. Add the stock, milk, parsley, salt and pepper and stir well to mix. Cover with the pastry and brush with a little beaten egg. Bake at 220°C/425°F/Gas Mark 7 for 30 minutes, and then at 190°C/375°F/Gas Mark 5 for 15 minutes. Serve with vegetables.

BACON AND EGG RAISED PIE
SERVES 8

$1\frac{1}{2}$ lb/675 g made shortcrust pastry (*see page 142*)
2 lb/900 g cooked bacon joint
1 egg, beaten
2 tablespoons concentrated tomato purée
2 tablespoons chopped parsley
pepper
3 hardboiled eggs
beaten egg for glazing
$\frac{1}{2}$ pint/300 ml aspic jelly

Use three-quarters of the pastry to line a 7 in/17.5 cm round cake tin with a removable base. Divide the bacon joint in half, and mince half finely. Mix the minced bacon with the beaten egg, tomato purée, parsley and pepper.

Chop the remaining bacon and 2 hardboiled eggs, and mix together. Line the pastry case with the minced mixture and fill with the chopped mixture, pushing the remaining whole egg into the centre. Cover with the remaining pastry and seal edges well. Make a small hole in the centre with a skewer, and brush well with beaten egg to glaze.

Bake at 200°C/400°F/Gas Mark 6 for 30 minutes. Cover with a double sheet of greaseproof paper and continue baking at 180°C/350°F/Gas Mark 4 for 1 hour. Leave in the tin to cool for 3 hours. Make up the aspic jelly from a packet and leave until cold and syrypy. Use a skewer to increase the size of hole in the lid and penetrate into the filling. Carefully spoon in the aspic jelly. Leave in a cold place for 3–4 hours until the pie is completely cold. Carefully remove from the tin and serve with salad or pickles. *Photographed on page 111*

CHEESE-TOPPED GAMMON
SERVES 4

4 gammon steaks
2 eating apples
a little melted butter
6 oz/175 g Cheddar or Edam cheese, thinly sliced

Derind the gammon steaks and snip the fat 4 or 5 times, so that they do not curl up.

Line a grill pan with foil and lay the steaks side by side on it. Grill 4–5 minutes each side.

Wipe and core the apples, but do not peel them, then slice thinly. Lay the apple slices across the bacon.

Brush a little melted butter over the apple slices and continue grilling for another 2–3 minutes. Lay the cheese slices over the apple and return to the grill for a further minute or so.

JAMBON MICHAUDIÈRE
SERVES 2

This fine ham dish is a speciality of the celebrated Chewton Glen Hotel restaurant in New Milton, Hampshire.

8 slices banana
a little marc de Bourgogne
8 oz/225 g made puff pastry (see page 142)
4 slices boiled ham, trimmed to fit the puff pastry (see below)
6 large plump prunes, stoned · 10 green grapes, peeled and pipped
egg yolk for glazing · 2 teaspoons Madeira

Place the banana slices in a small bowl, pour over the marc, toss gently and leave to marinate for a little while.

Divide the pastry into four equal-sized pieces and roll each out to an oval shape approximately $3 \times 1\frac{1}{2}$ in/7.5 × 4 cm. Place a slice of ham on two of them, in the centre. On top, arrange the marinated banana, the prunes and green grapes. Place over this the other slices of ham, but leave the edges clear. Moisten these with a little water and press down to seal.

Brush the pastry with egg yolk, decorate with the pastry trimmings and glaze again. Cook in a moderately hot oven, 200°C/400°F/Gas Mark 6 for 20–25 minutes. When ready, make a hole in the top and pour in the Madeira.

Serve with apple sauce (page 137) and Duchesse potatoes.

BACON AND PRAWN CREOLE
SERVES 4

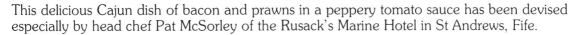

This delicious Cajun dish of bacon and prawns in a peppery tomato sauce has been devised especially by head chef Pat McSorley of the Rusack's Marine Hotel in St Andrews, Fife.

8 oz/225 g unsmoked bacon, cut into 2 in/5 cm strips
8 oz/225 g peeled scampi
2 oz/50 g onion, thinly sliced
1 chilli pepper, chopped
1 garlic clove, crushed
2 tablespoons butter
2 oz/50 g thinly sliced peppers, a mixture of red, yellow and green, if possible
15 oz/425 g can of peeled plum tomatoes, liquidised
4 fl oz/100 ml double cream
salt and pepper to taste
8 oz/225 g long grain or wild rice, cooked
chopped spring onions for garnish

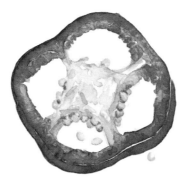

Toss the bacon, scampi, onion, chilli pepper and garlic in a saucepan over a moderate-to-high heat for a couple of minutes to seal them. Then add the sliced peppers and tomato purée and bring to a boil. Add the cream and simmer gently for 5 minutes. Season with salt and pepper to taste.

Serve on a bed of cooked rice and garnish with the chopped spring onions.

LITTLE GAMMON AND ARTICHOKE PIES
SERVES 6

A crisp, buttery puff pastry crust is the perfect accompaniment for this mixture of earthy artichokes and gammon, intriguingly sweetened with dates.

1 lb/450 g Jerusalem artichokes
2 tablespoons butter
2 tablespoons plain flour
$\frac{1}{2}$ pint/300 ml single cream, scalded and infused with a slice of onion and a bay leaf
Dijon mustard
salt and pepper
4 tablespoons each grated Gruyère and Parmesan cheese
1 lb/450 g made puff pastry (see page 142)
1 egg, beaten, for glazing
1 lb/450 g lean cooked gammon, diced
2 hardboiled eggs, quartered
6 fresh dates, stoned and chopped
chopped fresh parsley

Steam the artichokes until just tender. Set aside, and reserve $\frac{1}{2}$ pint/300 ml of the cooking liquid. Make a sauce, just as you would the white sauce on page 128, with the butter, flour, artichoke liquid and cream. Simmer to a good consistency and season with a teaspoon of mustard, and salt and pepper to taste. Add the grated cheese.

Defrost the puff pastry and roll out. Cut into 6 ovals, or rounds, using an upturned individual pie dish as a template.

Glaze with the beaten egg and bake on a dampened baking sheet for 15 minutes in a very hot oven, 230°C/450°F/Gas Mark 8, until puffed up, golden and crisp.

Meanwhile, chop the artichokes and add to the sauce with the gammon, eggs, dates and parsley. Heat through gently but thoroughly. Spoon the mixture into warmed pie dishes and top with the pastry lids.

Serve with leaf spinach, peas, French beans or a green salad.

SCALLOPED HAM WITH MUSHROOMS AND CHEESE
SERVES 4

Leftovers from a baked ham are ideal for making a dish such as this. Always allow a little more than the recipe says, to compensate for cutting away any skin.

generous $\frac{1}{2}$ pint/300 ml white sauce (see page 128)
pinch of ground nutmeg
2 oz/50 g butter
3 shallots, chopped, or 3 tablespoons chopped onion
6 oz/175 g button mushrooms, quartered
12 oz/350 g cooked ham, diced
2 oz/50 g grated Gruyère or Cheddar cheese
1 oz/25 g fresh breadcrumbs

Flavour the white sauce with nutmeg. Melt the butter and cook the shallots or onion gently until golden and soft. Add the mushrooms, and when cooked stir into the white sauce with the diced ham. Divide among 4 deep scallop shells or small fireproof pots.

Mix the cheese and breadcrumbs and scatter evenly over the ham mixture, dot with butter, and put in a very hot oven, 230°C/450°F/Gas Mark 8, or under the grill until brown and bubbling.

The dish can be prepared entirely in advance, with only the reheating in the oven or under the grill to be done at the last moment.

Serve with wholemeal brown bread. *Photographed on page 69*

HAM CROQUETTES
SERVES 4

2 oz/50 g butter, plus a little extra for frying
2 oz/50 g plain flour
$\frac{3}{4}$ pint/450 ml milk
4 oz/100 g mushrooms, chopped
8 oz/225 g ham
2 egg yolks
salt, pepper, and mace or nutmeg
flour, beaten egg and breadcrumbs to finish
oil for deep frying

Make a white sauce with the first three ingredients (see page 128), but leave it on a low heat to reduce by half – you should end up with a very thick 8 oz/225 g.

Cook the mushrooms in a little butter. Mince the ham twice, or process it finely in a food processor, and add it to the mushrooms.

Add the ham mixture to the white sauce, when it has reduced to the right amount, and sieve it or purée it in a blender. Reheat to just under boiling point, add the egg yolks, beating them in well for 2–3 minutes.

Pour the mixture into a buttered shallow dish to cool.

When you want to serve the croquettes, cut the mixture into even pieces, shape them into cylinders, roll them lightly in flour, then in egg, then in breadcrumbs; and fry quickly to golden brown in deep boiling oil. A chip basket helps.

Serve with Madeira sauce (page 134) or tomato sauce (page 135), and a selection of vegetables.

Ham croquettes, with tomato sauce (page 135),
gammon with pineapple (overleaf), and scalloped ham with mushrooms
and cheese (page 67)

REGIONAL DISHES, PARTY PIECES & BUFFETS

GAMMON WITH PINEAPPLE
SERVES 4

about 1 oz/25 g butter
4 gammon steaks
5 slices fresh, peeled pineaple
3 tablespoons Madeira
1 tablespoon sugar
1 teaspoon ground cinnamon
1 teaspoon arrowroot
watercress to garnish

Melt the butter in a shallow, fireproof dish. Turn over the gammon slices in the butter, then put 4 of the pineapple slices on top. Chop the extra slice roughly and cook it in about $\frac{1}{4}$ pint/150 ml water. When tender, remove from the heat and add the Madeira. Pour, with any pineapple juice collected when cutting the slices, into the gammon dish.

Mix the sugar with the cinnamon and sprinkle a little over the pineapple slices. You may not need it all. Bake in a moderate oven, 180°C/350°F/Gas Mark 4, until bubbling and tender, basting occasionally, for 20 minutes.

Spoon off the juice and boil it down to reduce by about half. Mix the arrowroot with 2 teaspoons cold water, add to the juices and cook gently until thickened and clear. Pour over and serve with watercress and fried potatoes. *Photographed on page 69*

REGIONAL DISHES, PARTY PIECES & BUFFETS

RIGODON BOURGIGNON
SERVES 4

In the days when every 'maison bourgeoise' in lower Burgundy had its bread oven, 'rigodon' was cooked after the bread on baking day. Half pudding, half omelette, it needs gentle heat.

7 oz/200 g cooked ham or bacon, thinly sliced
1 pint/600 ml milk
5 eggs, beaten
1½ oz/40 g flour
salt and pepper
pinch of ground allspice
pinch of thyme
1 oz/25 g butter

Cut the ham or bacon into tiny dice. If using bacon, fry it for 2–3 minutes in a frying pan until the fat runs but the bacon is not yet crisp. Butter a shallow 3 pint/1.5 l baking dish and sprinkle the ham or bacon over the bottom. Set the oven at moderate, 175°C/350°F/Gas Mark 4.

Bring the milk to a boil in a medium-sized saucepan. In a bowl, whisk the eggs and flour until smoth; gradually add the hot milk, whisking vigorously so that the milk does not cook the eggs. Season with salt, pepper, allspice and thyme.

Pour the mixture into the baking dish, dot with the butter and bake in the heated oven for 35–40 minutes or until set and golden brown; a knife inserted into the mixture should be dry when withdrawn. Serve rigodon from the dish, either warm or at room temperature, accompanied by a green salad.

BACON OLIVES IN LEMON SAUCE
SERVES 4

12 large back bacon rashers
a little fat for frying
6 oz/175 g long grain rice

Stuffing
1 oz/25 g butter
1 onion, finely chopped
2 oz/50 g fresh breadcrumbs
1 tablespoon chopped parsley
grated rind of $\frac{1}{2}$ lemon
salt and pepper

Sauce
1 oz/25 g butter
1 oz/25 g plain flour
$\frac{1}{2}$ pint/300 ml chicken stock
grated rind and juice of $\frac{1}{2}$ lemon

Remove the rind and spread out the rashers on a board. Make up the stuffing and divide it between the rashers. Roll them up neatly and tie each with string.

Melt a little fat and fry the stuffed rashers until they are lightly brown all over, turning frequently; reduce the heat and cook for a further 10 minutes, in all about 15 minutes.

Cook and drain the rice. Make the sauce by melting the butter, add the flour, cook for 1 minute, then gradually stir in the stock. Bring to a boil, stirring. Add the lemon juice and rind and cook for a further 2 minutes.

Serve the bacon olives on the rice and spoon over the sauce.

HAM IN PARSLEY JELLY
SERVES 8–10

This is one of the great classic dishes from the Burgundy region of France, where it is traditionally served at Easter. Its striking appearance – the pink ham contrasting with the green-flecked jelly – makes it the ideal party dish. The veal bones and pig's trotters are essential to give the jelly a good flavour and to set it. You can if you wish incorporate their meat into this dish, or keep them and serve them at some later time.

3–4 lb/1.35–2 kg unsmoked ham or gammon joint
2 calf's feet or pig's trotters, split
1 lb/450 g veal bones, cracked
bouquet garni: 2 bay leaves, 2 sprigs each parsley and thyme, 10 peppercorns
1 pint/600 ml dry white wine
6 shallots, finely chopped
about 2 tablespoons wine vinegar
large bunch of parsley, finely chopped

Into a large, heavy pan put the ham, calf's or pig's feet and veal bones, together with the bouquet garni, all but 4 fl oz/100 ml of the wine, and the shallots. Add enough water just to cover. Bring slowly to simmering point and cook at this rate until the ham is tender enough to be pierced easily with a fork – 2½–3 hours, or longer if necessary. Skim the surface of the liquid often during cooking to remove any scum or fat that rises to the surface and keep the mixture clear. Add more liquid if necessary (wine or water) to keep the meat covered.

When the meat is ready, remove it to a board. Remove the skin and discard it. Remove the meat from the calf's feet or pig's trotters and reserve it.

Boil the cooking liquid to reduce it to about 3 pints/1.5 l. Cut or pull the meat into chunks about 2 in/5 cm in size and mix it with wine vinegar to taste, the shallots and enough of the chopped parsley to give it a strong, but not overwhelming, green colour. Remove and discard the bouquet garni.

Strain the cooking liquid through dampened muslin and taste for seasoning. Place a layer of meat in a deep bowl or a terrine. Spoon over a covering layer of liquid. Leave until it is cool and beginning to set. Repeat these layers until the meat is used up and finish with the last of the jelly. Refrigerate for at least 3 hours or until set firm. The chilled dish will keep well.

To serve, run a sharp pointed knife around the edge of the bowl and unmould onto a platter. Serve with a green salad. *See frontispiece*

VENISON AND BACON ROULADE
SERVES 4

This grand dinner party dish combines bacon with one of Scotland's finest delicacies, venison, and has been created by Colin Chalmers, head chef at the Atholl Palace Hotel, Pitlochry, Perthshire.

2 oz/50 g butter
1 garlic clove, crushed
1 onion, finely chopped
4 oz/100 g button mushrooms, sliced
8 oz/225 g bacon, derinded and finely chopped
12 oz/350 g lean venison, finely chopped
pinch of thyme
freshly ground black pepper
1 lb/450 g made puff pastry (see page 142)
beaten egg for glazing
Madeira sauce (see page 134)

Melt the butter in a frying pan and fry together the garlic, onion, mushrooms, bacon, venison and thyme for about 10 minutes until the vegetables are soft and the meat browned on all sides. Season to taste with black pepper.

Roll out the puff pastry thinly to a rectangle, about 12×10 in/30×25 cm. With the shorter end facing you, spread the filling in a broad strip along the centre of the pastry leaving about $3\frac{1}{2}$ in/10 cm free all around. Slanting them towards you, make diagonal cuts right through the pastry, at 1 in/2.5 cm intervals along both sides. Brush with beaten egg. Turn the pastry up and over the filling neatly at the far end, then fold over the pastry strips, alternately left and right, to make a plait which will enclose the filling. Remember to tuck over and under the near end before finishing the 'plait'. Brush with beaten egg to glaze all over.

Bake the roulade in a hot oven, 220°C/425°F/Gas Mark 7, for 10 minutes, then lower the heat to 190°C/375°F/Gas Mark 5, and continue to bake for a further 30 minutes. This will give a crisp finish to the pastry and finish cooking the filling.

Serve with Madeira sauce (page 134) and Duchesse potatoes.

Two classic Scottish dishes, venison and bacon roulade, served with duchesse potatoes, and ham and haddie (page 49)

GAMMON IN PUFF PASTRY
SERVES 6

This makes a most impressive celebratory luncheon or dinner centrepiece. It needs, however, to be prepared over two days, so allow yourself plenty of time.

3 lb/1.5 kg gammon joint
chopped root vegetables (carrots, onions, leeks)
whole peppercorns
whole cloves
1 lb/450 g made puff pastry (see page 142)
1 egg for glazing, lightly beaten

Place the gammon joint in a large saucepan. Cover with fresh cold water, add the prepared vegetables and flavourings and cook as described in the master recipe for boiled bacon on page 9. When it is ready, remove the pan from the heat and leave the gammon to cool overnight in its liquid.

Next day, remove the gammon from the cooking liquid and carefully remove the skin. Roll out the puff pastry to an oblong shape and large enough to enclose the joint completely. Preheat the oven to 230°C/450°F/Gas Mark 8.

Place the gammon in the centre of the puff pastry sheet, brush the edges with a little of the beaten egg and pull them gently up and over the top of the gammon. Press the edges together well and carefully to enclose the meat and seal the edges. Lift the gammon and place it, seam side down, on a wet baking tray.

Brush the pastry all over with egg. Decorate the joint with the puff patry trimmings and glaze again.

Bake the gammon for 20 minutes in the preheated oven; lower the heat to 180°C/350°F/Gas Mark 4 and continue cooking for another 30 minutes. Cover the joint with dampened greaseproof paper when it has coloured enough.

This joint is equally good hot or cold.

Ham with a Fresh Cream Sauce
SERVES 6

This exceedingly good dish has a rich sauce, suitable for the grandest supper. If you wish, the lighter crème fraîche* can be substituted for the plain cream suggested here.

6 medium–thick (about $\frac{1}{4}$ in/$\frac{1}{2}$ cm) slices cooked ham
1 oz/25 g butter
1 oz/25 g chopped spring onions
$\frac{1}{4}$ pint/150 ml dry white wine
about 12 fl oz/350 ml cream
2 tablespoons French mustard
1 tablespoon tomato purée
4 oz/100 g button mushrooms, finely sliced
freshly ground black pepper

Trim the ham slices and fry them gently in the butter until lightly browned on both sides. Remove and keep warm. In the remaining fat, fry the spring onions slowly for 2–3 minutes. Pour in the wine, stir up the juices with a wooden spatula or spoon, turn up the heat and cook rapidly until the liquid has reduced to about 4 tablespoons.

Add the cream to the pan, blend in well the mustard and tomato purée, stir in the mushrooms and season with black pepper. Simmer slowly for 10–15 minutes, until the sauce has reduced and thickened slightly. Pour over the ham slices.

Serve with new potatoes.

*If you cannot get crème fraîche, you can substitute with Greek yoghurt. If you want to make your own crème fraîche, mix 1 tablespoon sour cream with $\frac{1}{4}$ pint/150 single cream in a little bowl. Leave in a warm place for 8 hours or so.

BAKED HAM CRUSTED WITH GROUND ALMONDS AND HYMETTUS HONEY
SERVES 20

8–10 lb/4–5 kg joint of cooked ham

Glaze
8 oz/225 g ground almonds
8–10 oz/225–275 g Hymettus or other fine-flavoured honey
grated zest of 1 lemon
$\frac{1}{2}$ teaspoon salt
$\frac{1}{2}$ teaspoon freshly ground pepper

Optional party-time extra
8 pieces candied pineapple, *or* slices fresh pineapple *or* drained tinned pineapple rings
8 glacé apricots

Having boiled or baked the piece of ham, if you have started from this point, remove the skin and some of the fat if there is a heavy cushion of this, whilst still hot.

Mix the ingredients for the glaze to a stiff paste, and spread this over the surface.

Stand the ham on a rack or piece of foil and put it in the oven, set at 200°C/400°F/ Gas Mark 6, for 25–30 minutes or until the glaze is well browned and cooked through (almonds burn easily so keep your eye on this). Leave to cool completely overnight.

Arrange the optional extras on top of the glaze before baking. Fix with wooden cocktail sticks. Dribble over a little extra honey, and sprinkle with salt and pepper.

Serve with Cumberland sauce (page 129) and a variety of salads.

BAKED BACON JOINT WITH RED BEANS AND SPICED APPLES
SERVES 6–8

8 oz/225 g dried red kidney beans *or* 1 can kidney beans
$2\frac{1}{2}$–3 lb/1.25–1.35 uncooked bacon joint
approx 8 cloves
a few peppercorns
2 oz/50 g butter
2 onions, chopped coarsely
1–2 cloves garlic, chopped finely
1 large cooking apple
$\frac{1}{2}$–1 teaspoon ground mace or nutmeg
1 tablespoon demerara sugar
$\frac{1}{4}$ pint/150 ml sweet or dry cider
salt and black pepper

If you are using dried kidney beans, soak them in cold water for 8 hours or overnight.

Press the cloves into the joint and put it in a large saucepan with a few peppercorns. Cover completely with water. Bring to the boil and then gently simmer for 1–$1\frac{1}{4}$ hours.

Meanwhile, boil the beans in unsalted water until soft ($\frac{3}{4}$–1 hour) and drain. Melt the fat in a pan and fry the onions until just soft. Stir in the chopped garlic. Then peel and thinly slice the apple and add to the pan, increasing the heat a little and tossing about for $\frac{1}{2}$–1 minute only – the apple must not go mushy. Stir in the mace or nutmeg and the cooked, or canned, drained beans, adding plenty of salt and black pepper. Keep warm in a covered bowl, in a low oven.

When the bacon is ready remove it from the pan and rinse. Heat the oven to 180°C/350°F/ Gas Mark 4. Remove the string from the bacon and cut or pull the skin from the joint. Score the fat in a diamond pattern and press the demerara sugar on to it. Put the joint into a roasting pan with the cider and cook in the centre of the oven for half an hour or until golden brown, basting now and then with the cider.

Put the joint on a large serving plate surrounded by the beans and apples and pour over any remaining juices.

HAM ROLLS STUFFED WITH TURKEY BREAST IN SPINACH SAUCE
SERVES 4

This is a simple, pretty and delectable dish. Serve it with new potatoes if possible, and baby carrots.

12 oz/350 g skinned turkey breast fillets
4 oz/100 g curd cheese
yolk of 1 large egg (size 1–2)
1 medium bunch of fresh chives, chopped or snipped finely with scissors
8 large slices cooked ham
butter
1 lb/450 g fresh spinach, chopped coarsely

Mince the turkey fillets or chop in a food processor. Mix thoroughly in a bowl with the curd cheese and the egg yolk. Stir the chopped chives into the mixture. Season with salt and pepper.

Lay out the slices of ham and spoon the mixture evenly towards the end of each piece. Roll each up from the shorter end and arrange the rolls closely together in an ovenproof dish. Smear them with softened butter and cover the dish with foil.

Put a large pan or dish, half-full of water, in the oven just below the centre and heat to 180°C/350°F/Gas Mark 4. Then put the dish of ham rolls in the pan of water and cook for 1 hour.

Pour the juices surrounding the rolls into a large saucepan. Cover the dish of rolls again and keep warm. Cook the spinach in the juices, with the pan covered, until tender. Season with pepper and then purée in a liquidiser or food processor until smooth. If the purée is very thick, add some butter. Spoon the purée roughly over the rolls just before serving.

BACON CASSOULET
SERVES 6–8

$2\frac{1}{2}$ lb/1.1 kg gammon or forehock joint
8 oz/225 g dried haricot beans
1 onion, peeled and chopped
2 medium carrots, peeled and chopped
bouquet garni: 6 parsley sprigs, 4 unpeeled garlic cloves, 2 cloves, sprig of fresh thyme
and 2 bay leaves tied in cheesecloth
2 tablespoons bacon fat, rendered, or lard
4 oz/100 g shallots or spring onions, sliced
4 oz/100 g red or green pepper, chopped
5 tablespoons tomato purée
$\frac{1}{2}$ pint/300 ml dry white wine or chicken stock
about 8 oz/225 g garlic sausage, thickly sliced
3 oz/75 g white breadcrumbs mixed with 4 tablespoons chopped parsley

Cover the bacon joint with cold water in a large saucepan, bring slowly to a boil, cover and simmer for 35 minutes. Remove from the heat and strip away the rind.

Meanwhile, drop the beans into boiling water. Bring quickly back to the boil and boil for 2 minutes. Remove from the heat and let the beans soak in the water for 1 hour.

Add the onion, carrots, and bouquet garni to the soaked beans and cook in the saucepan gently for 1 hour, adding more water as required. When the beans and vegetables are tender, the liquid should all have been absorbed by the beans.

Heat a little of the bacon fat or lard in a heavy, fireproof casserole and gently fry the shallots and peppers for 3 minutes. Cut the bacon joint into chunks roughly 2 in/5 cm square. Put in the bacon chunks also and brown these on all sides.

Stir in the tomato purée, white wine or stock and sliced garlic sausage. Spread over the crumbs and parsley and sprinkle the fat on top.

Bring the casserole to simmering point on top of the stove, then place it in the upper part of a moderately hot oven, 190°C/375°F/Gas Mark 5. When the crust has crusted lightly, in about 20 minutes, turn the oven down to 180°C/350°F/Gas Mark 4. Break the crust with the back of a serving spoon and baste it with the cooking liquid. Repeat several times as the crust forms again, but leave intact for the last 15 minutes or so of cooking. The cassoulet should be baked for about 1 hour in all. If the liquid in the casserole becomes too thick, add a little extra stock.

Serve the cassoulet from its casserole, with a simple side salad.

GAMMON STEAK WITH POACHED PEAR AND GINGER
SERVES 2

This original dish has been devised by David Sherratt, head chef at The Bull in Long Melford, Suffolk. For those of us who would prefer a less rich version, he suggests substituting dry white wine for the ginger wine, and reducing the amount of cream and stem ginger used here.

2 ripe, fresh pears
$\frac{1}{2}$ pint/300 ml ginger wine
2 oz/50 g butter
2 gammon steaks, trimmed
$\frac{1}{4}$ pint/150 ml white sauce (see page 128)
$\frac{1}{4}$ pint/150 ml whipping cream
2 pieces preserved stem ginger
watercress sprigs for garnish

Place the whole pears, ginger wine and half the butter in a deep saucepan. Cover with a lid and bring to a boil; lower the heat and simmer for about 10 minutes or until the pears are just tender. Remove the pears from the pan and cool them quickly in iced water. Bring the poaching liquid back to the boil and boil until reduced by half.

Melt the rest of the butter in a large frying pan, but do not allow it to colour. Add the gammon steaks and cook them quickly for a few minutes on each side to seal in the juices. Reduce the heat and add the reduced poaching liquid, the white sauce and the cream. Bring to the boil, then simmer for 2–3 minutes.

Peel and core the cooked pears and cut them in half lengthways. Keep one half of each pear to one side, and finely slice the other half. Add the ginger and sliced pear to the sauce, return to the heat and cook gently until the gammon is tender. Then remove the gammon from the pan and keep warm.

Bring the sauce to the boil and reduce it until it begins to thicken. With the two remaining pear halves, make a series of cuts starting about $\frac{1}{4}$ in/$\frac{1}{2}$ cm from the stem end and open each out to form a fan. Arrange one fan of pear on each gammon steak and coat them with the sauce. Garnish with watercress sprigs and serve at once.

Dome of ham and cucumber (overleaf), and gammon steak with poached pear
and ginger, served with a carrot and spinach mousse (page 124)

DOMES OF HAM AND CUCUMBER
SERVES 6

These elegant pastry domes filled with gammon are a speciality of John Benson Smith, head chef at The Black Swan in Helmsley, North Yorkshire.

12 oz/350 g made puff pastry (see page 142)
4 oz/100 g butter, plus a little extra for greasing
5 oz/150 g mushrooms, chopped into $\frac{1}{2}$ in/1 cm pieces
1 large onion, cut into $\frac{1}{2}$ in/1 cm dice
1$\frac{1}{2}$ lb/675 g lean cooked gammon, cut into $\frac{1}{2}$ in/1 cm dice
2 oz/50 g plain flour, sifted
$\frac{1}{2}$ pint/300 ml chicken stock
$\frac{1}{2}$ pint/300 ml double cream
pinch of fennel seeds
bunch of chives, finely chopped
1 oz/25 g parsley, finely chopped
1 cucumber, cut into $\frac{1}{2}$ in/1 cm dice
2 oz/50 g cooked chopped spinach
salt and freshly ground black pepper
lemon juice
ground nutmeg
1 garlic clove, crushed
egg yolk for glazing
chopped fresh herbs and thinly sliced red pepper for garnish

Roll out the puff pastry thinly and cut out from it 6 shapes to fit the inside of 6 round 3 in/ 7.5 cm diameter ovenproof dishes, and 6 circles to form lids. Place these in the refrigerator to chill for 10 minutes or so. Grease the dishes themselves.

Meanwhile, melt the butter in a saucepan, and add the mushrooms, onion and gammon. Cook until the vegetables are tender. Remove from the heat, mix in the flour, cover with a lid and place in a hot oven, 220°C/425°F/Gas Mark 7, for 3 minutes. Remove, cool slightly, then gradually incorporate the chicken stock and double cream. Return to the boil, add in the fennel seeds, chives, parsley, cucumber and spinach and simmer over a gentle heat for 15 minutes. Season to taste and leave until cool.

Line the moulds with the puff pastry. Half-fill them with the gammon mixture and reserve any excess. Brush the inside of the pastry lids with egg yolk and place them on top of the domes. Crimp them around the edge to form a seal. Bake the domes in a hot oven, 230°C/450°F/Gas Mark 8, for 10–15 minutes. Remove, leave to cool slightly then, with the help of a small knife, free each pastry dome from its dish and turn them upside down on a baking tray. Brush with egg yolk again and return to the oven for a further 5 minutes to colour the pastry golden-brown.

Cover the base of 6 serving plates with any excess gammon mixture, processed to make a sauce and reheated. Carefully place a dome in the centre of each. Decorate with chopped fresh herbs and sliced red pepper and serve. *Photographed on page 83*

BOILED BACON AND CABBAGE
SERVES 4

This economical yet delicious and deeply satisfying dish makes the most of two natural partners. The exchange of flavours allowed by the long slow cooking lifts the down-to-earth cabbage into another class.

$2\frac{1}{2}$ lb/1.1 kg forehock or gammon joint
1 large head of firm cabbage, trimmed
6 oz/175 g carrots, peeled and sliced
6 peppercorns
1 bay leaf
chicken stock

Put the bacon into a saucepan, cover with water, bring slowly to a boil and simmer for 30 minutes. Drain and pare off the rind.

Quarter the cabbage, without quite cutting it through. Take a fireproof casserole just large enough to take the bacon and cabbage. Put in the cabbage and spread it out a little to make a bed for the bacon joint. Place the carrots, peppercorns and bay leaf on top. Add enough stock or water to cover, put a lid on top and simmer, either over a low heat on top of the cooker or in a slow oven, 150°C/300°F/Gas Mark 2, for 2 hours or until the bacon and cabbage are tender. Stir occasionally to prevent the cabbage sticking to the bottom of the pan. Add more stock or water while the casserole is cooking, if it becomes necessary.

Remove the bacon from the pan, cut into thick slices and serve surrounded by the cabbage.

BUCKINGHAMSHIRE BADGER
SERVES 6

12 oz/350 g self-raising flour
6 oz/175 g shredded suet
salt and pepper
8 oz/225 g liver, finely chopped
8 oz/225 g streaky bacon rashers, finely chopped
1 large onion, finely chopped
3 teaspoons chopped fresh sage

Prepare the pastry by stirring together flour, suet and a pinch of salt until evenly mixed. Add just enough cold water to make a firm dough. Roll out on a floured board into a rectangle about 10 × 15 in/25 × 37.5 cm.

Mix the liver, bacon and onion and stir in the sage. Season well with salt and pepper. Arrange on the pastry and roll up like a Swiss roll. Tie into a floured cloth and place in a pan of boiling water. Boil for 2 hours. Unroll carefully on a serving dish, and serve with gravy and vegetables.

BRITHYLL A CIG MOCH
SERVES 4

In other words, trout with bacon in the Welsh style.

approx 6 oz/175 g streaky bacon rashers
4 rainbow trout, weighing about 8 oz/225 g each, cleaned
chopped parsley
salt and freshly ground black pepper

Take a pie or gratin dish, and line it with the rashers of bacon, smoked or unsmoked, according to the flavour you prefer.

Season the fish, and arrange them head to tail on the bacon. Sprinkle with chopped parsley, salt and freshly ground black pepper. Fold any long ends of bacon round and over the trout.

Bake, covered, for about 20 minutes in a moderate oven, 180°C/350°F/Gas Mark 4. The time depends on the size of the fish.

If you are just cooking a couple of fish, it is more sensible to wrap each one in two rashers of bacon. Lining a whole dish would be too much.

Serve with new potatoes and peas.

WELSH PASTIES
SERVES 6–8

Pastry
8 oz/225 g plain flour
pinch of onion salt
3 oz/75 g butter
3 oz/75 g cream cheese

Filling
2 medium leeks, thinly sliced
4 oz/100 g cold boiled bacon, finely chopped
1 tablespoon chopped fresh parsley
pepper
4 tablespoons thick white sauce (see page 128)
2 teaspoons lemon juice
beaten egg for glazing

Prepare the pastry by sieving the flour and salt into a bowl, and then rubbing in the butter and cream cheese. Press the mixture into a soft dough, wrap in foil and chill until firm. Roll out and cut into eight 4 in/10 cm circles.

Cook the leeks in boiling salted water until just tender, and drain very well, pressing out excess liquid. Mix the leeks, bacon, parsley and pepper into the white sauce and add the lemon juice. Leave until completely cold. Put a spoonful on each pastry circle and moisten the edges with beaten egg. Bring up the edges to meet on top and pinch them together firmly. Brush with beaten egg. Bake at 200°C/400°F/Gas Mark 6 for 20 minutes. Serve hot with vegetables or cold with salad.

BACON AND CHEESE PASTIES
SERVES 6

1 lb/450 g made shortcrust pastry (see page 142)
1 medium onion, finely chopped
4 oz/100 g back bacon rashers, finely chopped
1 oz/25 g butter
1 large cooking apple, peeled, cored and finely chopped
4 oz/100 g grated Cheddar cheese
salt and pepper · beaten egg for glazing

Roll out the pastry and cut into eight 6 in/15 cm circles. Put the onion, bacon and butter into a small pan and cook over low heat for 5 minutes, stirring well. Remove from the heat. Add the apple to the onion mixture with the cheese, and season well with salt and pepper.

Place a spoonful of filling in the centre of each pastry circle and pull up the edges, sealing with thumb and finger. Brush with beaten egg to glaze. Place on a baking sheet, and bake at 190°C/375°F/Gas Mark 5 for 25 minutes. Serve hot or cold.

BACON AND KIDNEY PASTIES
SERVES 6

1 lb/450 g made shortcrust pastry (see page 142)
8 oz/225 g raw lean steak, minced
6 oz/175 g streaky bacon rashers, finely chopped
4 oz/100 g lambs' kidneys, finely chopped
1 large onion, finely chopped
$\frac{1}{2}$ teaspoon Worcestershire sauce · salt and pepper

Roll out the pastry and cut into six 7 in/17.5 cm circles. Mix the steak, bacon, kidneys and onion and season with sauce, salt and pepper. Put the mixture on to half of each circle and fold over pastry. Press the edges together with a fork. Brush with a little beaten egg. Bake at 220°C/425°F/Gas Mark 7 for 15 minutes, and then at 180°C/350°F/Gas Mark 4 for 40 minutes. Serve hot with gravy, vegetables and potatoes, or cold with salad.

Three West Country favourites, bacon and cheese pasty, Somerset cider gammon (overleaf), and Wiltshire bacon scones (page 141)

TREACLE BAKED BACON
SERVES 8–12

$2\frac{1}{2}$–3 lb/1.35–1.3 kg gammon or forehock joint
$\frac{1}{4}$ teaspoon allspice berries and $\frac{1}{4}$ teaspoon cloves, *or* just $\frac{1}{2}$ teaspoon cloves
$\frac{1}{4}$–$\frac{1}{2}$ teaspoon black peppercorns
black treacle · demerara sugar

Put the spices and peppercorns in a liquidiser or coffee grinder and whizz up until roughly ground. Mix them with enough black treacle to smear thickly all over the bacon joint. Wrap up well in two or three layers of foil. Put in a roasting tin and cook in a low oven, 140°C/275°F/Gas Mark 1 for 3–4 hours, according to size. Remove from the oven, unwrap, cut off the thick bacon skin while still hot and pour off any juices. Wrap again in foil, put heavy books or weights on top and leave to cool for 12 hours or overnight.

Then chill in the fridge and when you unwrap the foil sprinkle demerara sugar thickly all over the fat where the skin was taken off. As with most cold meats, this is most delicious if carved as thinly as possible.

Ideal for a party, this aromatic piece of meat will keep well, foil-wrapped in the fridge.

SOMERSET CIDER GAMMON
SERVES 4

4 gammon steaks
2 teaspoons made mustard
2 dessert apples, peeled and thinly sliced
$\frac{1}{4}$ pint/150 ml dry cider
pinch of fresh thyme · salt and pepper

Derind the gammon steaks. Spread on both sides with mustard. Grill on both sides until lightly browned. Take 4 large squares of foil and place a piece of gammon on each one. Top with apple slices. Take any fat drippings from the grill pan and pour over the apples. Add the cider and form the foil into parcels. Place on a baking sheet and bake at 200°C/400°F/Gas Mark 6 for 30 minutes.

Carefully slide the gammon steaks on to a serving plate and pour over the juices. Serve with vegetables and potatoes. *Photographed on page 89*

REGIONAL DISHES, PARTY PIECES & BUFFETS

PILGRIM'S GAMMON
SERVES 4

Martin Wickham, head chef at The Chaucer in Canterbury, created this dish especially to take advantage of the fine Kentish Pilgrim's cider. If you do not have any of this to hand, your own local cider will do very well provided it is good and dry.

4 gammon steaks
1 pint/600 ml Pilgrim's or other dry local cider
2 English dessert apples, peeled, cored and sliced
pinch of ground cinnamon
2 oz/50 g light soft brown sugar
4 slices fresh pineapple
2 tomatoes
watercress sprigs

Score around the edges of the gammon steaks, to prevent them from curling up when cooking. Heat the cider in a deep saucepan and put in the apple slices, cinnamon and sugar. Simmer together gently until the apple is tender.

Meanwhile, place the gammon steaks on a rack over a deep grill pan and quickly grill them for a few minutes on each side to brown them and seal in the flavours.

Place a slice of pineapple on top of each gammon steak, and pour over the cider and apple mixture. Put back under the grill and continue cooking the gammon. While this is happening the liquid in the grill pan will be reducing; when there is only a small amount of liquid left – say about 6 tablespoons – remove the gammon to a warmed serving dish and pour over the cooking juices.

To prepare the tomato garnish, take each one and hold it between the thumb and forefinger and, using a small sharp knife, make zigzag cuts around the middle; then carefully separate the two halves. Arrange these around the gammon, with a watercress sprig in the centre of each.

BELL TOURNEDOS WITH BACON AND PRAWNS
SERVES 2

Grand enough to be the centrepiece of a celebration dinner for two, this recipe is the creation of George Price, head chef at the Bell Hotel in Thetford, Norfolk.

4 oz/100 g butter
1 tablespoon oil
2 × 5 oz/150 g tournedos
(beef fillet steaks 1 in/2.5 cm thick, wrapped in strips of pork fat)
2 slices white bread, crusts removed
4 oz/100 g back bacon, diced
2 oz/50 g cooked peeled prawns
4 tablespoons dry sherry
4 tablespoons double cream
salt and freshly ground black pepper
2 sprigs parsley for garnish

Heat the butter with the oil in a heavy-based frying pan, over a moderate heat. When the butter and oil foam, put in the tournedos and cook them until done to your taste (as a guide, 3–4 minutes each side will give you a medium-rare steak). When ready, remove the tournedos to 2 plates and keep warm while you finish the sauce.

Cut from each slice of bread a circle about 2 in/5 cm across and fry these on both sides in the fat until golden. Remove, and place under the tournedos. In their place, put the bacon and prawns, cook them for a few minutes to heat through then put them on top of the tournedos.

Pour out the fat from the frying pan. Stir in the sherry and boil it over a high heat, scraping up the cooking juices as you do so, until it has reduced by about half. Add the cream, stir together and reduce again for 2–3 minutes. Check the seasoning. Pour the sauce around the steaks and serve at once, each one garnished with a sprig of parsley.

LE SAUPIQUET
SERVES 4

This is a modern version of a very old and famous speciality from the Burgundy region of France. It is said that its name comes from 'pique de sel' meaning 'spiced with salt'. Whatever its origins, it is the best and most delectable way of reheating cooked ham.

4 thick slices cooked ham, weighing about 4 oz/100 g each

Saupiquet sauce
5 shallots, very finely chopped
4 juniper berries, crushed
3 fl oz/75 ml wine vinegar
3 oz/75 g butter
1 oz/25 g plain flour
$\frac{1}{2}$ pint/300 ml hot beef or veal stock
$\frac{1}{4}$ pint/150 ml dry white wine
5 black peppercorns, crushed
about $\frac{1}{4}$ pint/150 ml double cream

Put the shallots, the juniper berries and wine vinegar into a small saucepan. Bring to a boil and cook until the liquid has almost completely evaporated.

In another saucepan, melt 1 oz/25 g of the butter, stir in the flour and cook over a gentle heat, stirring, until the mixture is coffee-coloured. Whisk in the hot stock gradually, then add the wine, the shallot mixture and the peppercorns. Simmer for about 30 minutes, skimming the sauce from time to time to remove any scum, then sieve it.

Return the sauce to a clean pan, stir in the cream, bring just up to the boil and taste for seasoning. Take off the heat and whisk in a knob of butter – about 1 oz/25 g – a piece at a time. Keep warm.

Heat the remaining butter in a frying pan and brown the ham slices lightly on each side. Transfer them to a heated platter, pour over some of the sauce and serve the rest separately.

Serve with crusty French bread and a green salad.

STUFFED HAM EN CROÛTE
SERVES 10

6 lb/3.7 kg boiled ham, skinned and trimmed of excess fat (*see basic recipe on page 9*)
1½ lb/675 g button mushrooms, chopped
1½ oz/40 g butter
2 teaspoons oil
1½ oz/40 g spring onions
3 tablespoons Madeira or dry sherry
salt and pepper
4 oz/100 g tinned chestnut purée
1½ lb/675 g made puff pastry (*see page 142*)
1 large egg, beaten, for glazing

Place the skinned and trimmed joint of cooked ham on a board. Using a long sharp knife, slice it, but not quite through so that it is still intact at the bottom and can be opened out rather like the leaves of a book.

Next make the stuffing. A handful at a time, twist the mushrooms in the corner of a clean drying-up cloth to extract their moisture. Fry them in the butter and oil, with the spring onions, for 8–10 minutes. Add the Madeira or sherry and boil rapidly until the liquid has almost completely evaporated. Transfer to a mixing bowl and season to taste. Stir in the chestnut purée and check the seasoning again – do not oversalt, as the ham will provde its own.

Carefully part the slices of ham and spread them with the stuffing. When finished, press the joint back into its original shape as much as possible. Preheat the oven to 210°C/425°F/Gas Mark 7.

Roll out two-thirds of the puff pastry into a circle about $\frac{1}{8}$in/$\frac{1}{4}$cm thick. Lay it on a baking sheet. Place the stuffed ham on it. Bring the pastry up around the ham and press it lightly into place. Roll out the rest of the dough and cut it to fit over the top of the joint. Brush the edge of the bottom pastry circle with beaten egg, and press the top circle into place. Flute or pinch the edges together to seal them. Brush the top of the pastry case with beaten egg. Use the pastry trimmings to make decorative leaves or other shapes, press these on to the pastry and glaze again.

Cook the ham en croûte in the preheated oven for 30 minutes or so, until nicely brown.

Serve with petits pois and baby carrots.

GAMMON STEAKS IN MADEIRA SAUCE
SERVES 4

4 gammon steaks
2 oz/50 g butter
1 large onion, thinly sliced
4–6 oz/100–175 g button mushrooms, stalks removed and roughly chopped
4 large tomatoes, skinned and roughly chopped
$\frac{1}{4}$ teaspoon dried basil
$\frac{1}{4}$ teaspoon dried marjoram
2 fl oz/50 ml Madeira
4 fl oz/100 ml ham stock or bouillon
salt and black pepper
1 teaspoon caster sugar
lemon juice

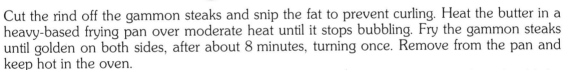

Cut the rind off the gammon steaks and snip the fat to prevent curling. Heat the butter in a heavy-based frying pan over moderate heat until it stops bubbling. Fry the gammon steaks until golden on both sides, after about 8 minutes, turning once. Remove from the pan and keep hot in the oven.

Fry the onion, mushroom caps and stalks lightly in the pan juices until softened; add the tomatoes, the basil and marjoram. Cover the pan with a lid or kitchen foil and simmer for about 5 minutes, shaking the pan from time to time.

Return the gammon steaks to the pan and add the Madeira, with enough stock almost to cover the meat. Season to taste with salt, freshly ground black pepper, sugar and lemon juice. Cover the pan again and continue cooking over low heat for 10 minutes or until the gammon is tender.

Arrange the steaks on a hot serving dish with the sauce poured over them. Baby sprouts, tossed in butter, and creamed potatoes or fluffy boiled rice, to mop up the sauce, would be good with the gammon.

A GLAZED HAM

A glazed ham makes a beautiful centrepiece for a buffet party. Small bacon joints may be treated the same way, but the glaze and decoration looks most attractive on a 10–15 lb/ 4.5–7 kg piece of meat, or on a 4–5 lb/2–2.5 kg corner or middle gammon. Calculate the total cooking time at 20 minutes per lb/450 g and 20 minutes over. Simmer the ham for half the total time and strip off the skin. Bake at 180°C/350°F/Gas Mark 4 until 20 minutes before the end of cooking time. Coat the fat with the glaze (and garnish if required). Finish baking at 220°C/425°F/Gas Mark 7 for 20 minutes, basting two or three times. Serve hot or cold.

GLAZING AND GARNISHING

When the skin has been stripped off, score the fat with a sharp knife to form diamonds. Brush with the glaze, and add garnish if used (see drawings on page 10). Bake for 20 minutes, basting well with the glaze which runs off the joint during cooking.

SUGAR AND CLOVE GLAZE   Mix 1 teaspoon ground cloves with 4 tablespoons dark soft brown sugar and mix to a paste with a little ginger ale. Spread on the fat and stick a clove into each diamond.

CIDER GLAZE   Pour $\frac{1}{2}$ pint/300 ml sweet cider over the fat. Sprinkle the top with 3 tablespoons demerara sugar and stick a clove into each diamond.

HONEY AND PINEAPPLE GLAZE   Pour $\frac{1}{2}$ pint/300 ml pineapple juice and 3 tablespoons white wine vinegar over the fat. Spread on 2 tablespoons clear honey and arrange a pineapple chunk in each diamond, fixed with a clove.

MARMALADE AND APPLE GLAZE   Spread 4 oz/100 g dark orange marmalade on the fat. Peel and core a large dessert apple. Slice thinly and dip slices in lemon juice. Secure in each diamond with a clove.

A glazed and decorated ham, served with spiced peaches (page 133), cranberry sauce (page 128) and Madeira sauce (page 134)

LE POUNTI
SERVES 6–8

Half meat loaf, half vegetable soufflé, *pounti* comes from the Auvergne region of France. This ham and spinach flan can also be flavoured with whole prunes or raisins.

5 oz/150 g bacon, chopped
4 oz/100 g cooked ham, chopped
1 onion, finely chopped
1 garlic clove, finely chopped
7 tablespoons chopped parsley
5 oz/150 g fresh spinach, chopped
3 oz/75 g plain flour
1 pint/600 ml milk
4 eggs
pinch of pepper

Mix together in a bowl the bacon, ham, onion, garlic, parsley and spinach. Set the oven at moderate, 180°C/350°F/Gas Mark 4.

Sift the flour into another bowl, make a well and gradually stir in the milk. Whisk in the eggs to make a batter and add the pepper. Stir the batter into the bacon mixture. Pour into a buttered shallow baking dish of about $2\frac{1}{2}$ pint/1.5 l capacity and bake for 50–60 minutes or until set.

Serve the *pounti* hot or at room temperature, cut in wedges like a cake.

HOT LITTLE NUMBERS
& COLD ONES TOO
MORSELS TO GO WITH DRINKS

Partygoers enjoy tasty little snacks to accompany their drinks, and only a boring hostess offers just crisps and nuts. Bacon and ham are always easy to buy and not expensive in the small quantities which can be turned into trays of cocktail party pieces for guests. While cold snacks are delicious and easy to prepare in advance, the successful hostess will always offer at least a couple of hot little numbers which stimulate the appetite as well as the conversation. These may also be prepared ahead for heating just before service. It is not necessary to provide a huge variety of snacks as these can be confusing and look unattractive when displayed – two or three cold pieces and a couple of hot ones will give all the necessary choice.

Allow at least two of each kind for every guest.

DEVILS ON HORSEBACK
SERVES 6–8

24 prunes, soaked
24 blanched almonds
6 streaky bacon rashers

When the prunes are very plump, drain them well. Make a slit in each one with a sharp knife and remove the stone. Put an almond into each prune. Derind the bacon and spread out each rasher thinly with a broad-bladed knife. Cut each rasher into four pieces. Wrap a piece of bacon round each prune. Grill under medium heat until the bacon is crisp on all sides. Spear on cocktail sticks to serve.

MUSSELS IN BACON WITH TARTARE DIP
SERVES 6–8

32 bottled mussels
8 streaky bacon rashers

Tartare dip
$\frac{1}{4}$ pint/150 ml mayonnaise
few drops of Tabasco sauce
1 tablespoon capers, finely chopped
1 tablespoon pickled gherkins, finely chopped

Drain the mussels very well. Derind the bacon and spread each rasher out thinly with a broad-bladed knife. Cut each rasher into four pieces. Wrap each mussel in a piece of bacon and grill under medium heat until the bacon is crisp on all sides. Spear on cocktail sticks and arrange on a serving dish round a bowl of tartare dip. Make this by seasoning the mayonnaise with Tabasco sauce and folding in the capers and gherkins.

COCKTAIL KEBABS

Cocktail sticks threaded with a variety of savoury tidbits are easy to serve with drinks. They may be simply arranged on a tray, or speared into a firm base such as a grapefruit or hard cabbage for an attractive presentation.

COLD KEBABS

1. Arrange alternating cubes of cheese, cooked ham and pineapple cubes on cocktail sticks.
2. Arrange alternating pieces of pineapple, ham and mandarin orange segments on sticks.
3. Arrange alternating cubes of ham, prawns and cucumber on cocktail sticks.

HOT KEBABS

1. Wrap tiny pieces of thin streaky bacon around prawns. Spear 3–4 on cocktail sticks and grill quickly to crisp the bacon.
2. Wrap pieces of thin streaky bacon around thick banana slices. Spear 2–3 pieces on cocktail sticks and finish with a piece of pineapple. Grill quickly to crisp the bacon.
3. Grill fish fingers until crisp and cooked. Cut into four pieces and wrap each one in a thin piece of streaky bacon lightly spread with tomato ketchup. Grill quickly to crisp the bacon.

SAUSAGES IN BACON ROLLS
MAKES 24

8 streaky bacon rashers
24 cocktail sausages
French mustard

Cut each rasher of bacon into 3, and stretch each piece lengthwise. Spread them with mustard. Wrap each sausage in the bacon and secure with a cocktail stick.

Bake the rolls in a hot oven, 210°C/425°F/Gas Mark 7, for 7 minutes or so. Serve right away, on their sticks.

CHICKEN LIVER AND BACON ROLLS
SERVES 6–8

8 oz/225 g chicken livers
8 streaky bacon rashers
French mustard

Cut each liver into four pieces. Derind the rashers and spread out the bacon thinly with a broad-bladed knife. Cut each rasher into 4 pieces and spread lightly with mustard. Wrap each piece of bacon round a piece of chicken liver, to make neat rolls. Place closely together in a roasting tin and cook at 180°C/350°F/Gas Mark 4 for 15 minutes. Drain well and spear on cocktail sticks for serving.

CURRIED MINI TURNOVERS
MAKES 18 TURNOVERS

1 lb/450 g made shortcrust pastry (see page 142)
6 oz/150 g cooked ham, finely chopped
3 tablespoons soured cream
2 tablespoons mayonnaise
2 tablespoons chopped chives
1 teaspoon curry powder
$\frac{1}{4}$ teaspoon mustard powder
salt and pepper
beaten egg for glazing

Roll out the pastry and cut into eighteen 3 in/7.5 cm circles. Mix the ham with all the other ingredients except the beaten egg. Put a little mixture on one side of each pastry circle. Fold over the pastry and seal the edges firmly. Prick the top of each turnover lightly two or three times with a fork. Brush the pastry with beaten egg to glaze. Put on a baking sheet and bake at 200°C/400°F/Gas Mark 6 for 20 minutes. Serve warm.

COCKTAIL QUICHES
MAKES 18 SMALL QUICHES

8 oz/225 g made shortcrust pastry (see page 142)
1 oz/25 g grated Parmesan cheese
4 back bacon rashers, finely chopped
$\frac{1}{4}$ pint/150 ml single cream
2 eggs and 2 egg yolks
pinch of mustard powder
few drops of Tabasco sauce
salt and pepper

Roll out the pastry and line 18 small tart tins. Prick the bases with a fork two or three times and bake blind at 200°C/400°F/Gas Mark 6 for 5 minutes. Remove from the oven and sprinkle immediately with the Parmesan cheese. Divide the chopped bacon between the pastry cases. Beat together the cream, eggs and egg yolks with the seasonings. Pour into the cases. Bake at 180°C/350°F/Gas Mark 4 for 20 minutes. Leave in tins for 5 minutes, then lift carefully on to a wire rack. Serve warm.

ANGELS ON HORSEBACK
SERVES 6–8

24 oysters
8 streaky bacon rashers

Derind the bacon and spread each rasher out thinly with a broad-bladed knife. Cut each rasher into three pieces. Wrap a piece of bacon round each oyster. Grill under medium heat until the bacon is crisp on all sides. Spear on cocktail sticks to serve. 'Angels' may be served as an after-dinner savoury if three or four are placed on a small slice of buttered toast, and sprinkled with a little cayenne pepper.

SPECIAL SAUSAGE ROLLS
MAKES 8 LARGE OR 16 SMALL SAUSAGE ROLLS

1 lb/450 g made puff pastry (see page 142)
8 large pork sausages
8 streaky bacon rashers
2 tablespoons mango chutney
beaten egg for glazing

Cut the pastry in two pieces and roll each piece to a strip approximately 16 × 16 in/40 × 40 cm. Skin the sausages and reshape them with floured hands. Derind the bacon and stretch the rashers with a broad-bladed knife. Chop any large pieces in the mango chutney and spread the chutney on the bacon. Wrap each sausage in a rasher and place four sausages on each strip of pastry.

Brush the pastry edges with beaten egg and fold over the sausages. Seal the edges firmly and cut each roll into 4 or 8 pieces. Brush with beaten egg. Place on a baking sheet and bake at 220°C/425°F/Gas Mark 7 for 25 minutes.

VOL-AU-VENT FILLINGS

Frozen vol-au-vent cases may be quickly baked, and may be prepared in advance of a party. The fillings may also be prepared in advance, and then may be inserted just before the little pastry cases are reheated for serving. Use the white sauce recipe on page 128 as a base, cooking it until it has become thick and creamy, and add the desired flavourings:

1   Chopped cooked ham and chopped cooked mushrooms, seasoned with a pinch of marjoram.
2   Add 1 oz/25 g grated cheese to the sauce and then fold in pieces of crisply grilled bacon.
3   Add a few pieces of cooked flaked smoked haddock with pieces of crisply grilled bacon.

From the top Special sausage rolls, vols-au-vent filled with ham and mushroom, ham and asparagus bundles (page 107), and crispy bacon balls (overleaf)

CRISPY BACON BALLS
MAKES 30 (approximately)

1 lb/450 g cooked bacon from a joint, *or* fresh rashers
2 medium onions, chopped
2 oz/50 g butter
2 oz/50 g plain flour
$\frac{1}{2}$ pint/300 ml chicken stock
freshly ground black pepper
6 oz/175 g fresh breadcrumbs
2 eggs, beaten
2 tablespoons French mustard
oil for deep frying

Cut up the bacon, and mince it together with the onion, or process them together.

Melt the butter in a heavy-based pan, stir in the flour and cook for 1–2 minutes to make a *roux*. Add the stock and stir until it comes to a boil. Cook for 2 minutes, stirring. Remove from the heat, season with pepper and add in two-thirds of the breadcrumbs. Bind this together with half the beaten eggs. Mix through well, with the minced bacon and onion and mustard.

Make small balls of the mixture and put them in the fridge for 30 minutes at least, to chill and become firm enough to handle easily.

Roll the balls in the rest of the beaten egg, and then in the remaining breadcrumbs. Deep-fry in hot oil for 7 minutes or so. *Photographed on page 105*

MORSELS TO GO WITH DRINKS

HAM AND ASPARAGUS BUNDLES
MAKES 24

24 spears fresh asparagus, cooked
8 oz/225 g thinly sliced cooked ham
freshly ground black pepper

Trim the tough stalks of the asparagus so that they measure about 3 in/7 cm, and pare any woody outer skin. Sprinkle with black pepper.

Cut the ham into strips about 2 in/5 cm wide and wrap these around the asparagus spears, leaving the tips exposed. *Photographed on page 105*

BACON BUTTER

This is a very good savoury butter perfect for spreading on cocktail biscuits or little toasts. Adjust the quantity given here according to your own needs, but the basic proportions are 4 oz/100 g cooked bacon, minced or processed with a shallot and mixed into an equal weight of softened unsalted butter and seasoned with black pepper.

Simply spread your chosen base with the bacon butter – quite thickly if you wish – and decorate it. Suitable accompaniments would be halved stoned olives, halved walnuts, or chopped hardboiled egg mixed with chopped watercress.

HAM AND HORSERADISH DIP
SERVES 6–8

8 oz/225 g cooked ham, finely minced
4 oz/100 g cream cheese
1 tablespoon grated horseradish
1 tablespoon chopped parsley
salt and pepper

Mix the ham with the cheese, horseradish and parsley and season to taste with salt and pepper. Beat well until light and creamy. Place in a serving bowl surrounded by crisps or small salted biscuits.

MINI CROQUE MONSIEUR
SERVES 6–8

8 thin slices white bread
8 thin slices Gruyère cheese
8 thin slices cooked ham
oil for shallow frying

Make sandwiches with a slice of cheese and ham in each. Cut off the crusts and press the edges together firmly. Fry in hot oil until crisp and golden on both sides. Lift out of the pan with an egg slice, draining well. Place on a piece of kitchen paper on a wire cake rack to absorb excess fat. Leave for 5 minutes and then cut carefully into quarters. Arrange on a serving dish and serve hot.

HAM CANAPÉS
MAKES 24

24 small rounds of white bread
(use a pastry cutter to make these)
3 oz/75 g cream cheese
6 tablespoons cream
2 tablespoons finely chopped chives
salt and freshly ground black pepper
about 6 thin slices ham
tinned red pimento or cocktail gherkins for garnish

Cut out the rounds of white bread and cook them, on a baking sheet in a hot oven, 210°C/425°F/Gas Mark 7, for 5 minutes on each side until dry and golden. Transfer to a wire rack and leave to cool.

In a bowl, combine the cream cheese, cream and chives. Season to taste. Divide up the slices of ham and shape each into a small neat roll. Spread the cream cheese mixture on the canapé bases, place a ham roll on each and garnish with a strip of tinned red pimento or cocktail gherkin.

HAM AND EGG CANAPÉS
MAKES 24

6 oz/175 g shelled hazelnuts
4 oz/100 g softened butter
24 toasted rounds of white bread (*see preceding recipe*) *or* plain cocktail crackers
about 6 slices cooked ham
6 hard-boiled eggs
chopped fresh parsley

Coarsely chop the hazelnuts. Add half the chopped nuts to the butter and mix well. Spread half of this nut butter over the toasted bread rounds or crackers.

Cut the slices of ham into circles the same size as the toasts or crackers. Save the trimmings (they can be used in a soufflé or omelette, for instance). Cut each egg into 8 slices.

Put a piece of ham onto each canapé. Arrange 2 slices of egg on top and scatter over the remaining chopped nuts and a little parsley. If you wish you could also use the ham trimmings here, simply by chopping them finely and sprinkling them over the top as well.

CRISP BACON AND EGG OPEN SANDWICH
MAKES 1 SANDWICH

3 streaky bacon rashers, derinded
1 slice pumpernickel bread
a little mayonnaise
1 hardboiled egg, sliced
1 slice tomato
watercress *or* cress

Fry or grill the bacon gently until crisp and drain on kitchen paper. Spread the bread with a little mayonnaise and arrange the egg on top in two rows so that it is covered. Lay the bacon on top. Cut the tomato slice through to its centre and shape it into a twist. Place on top of the bacon and garnish with watercress or cress.

HAM CORNETS

These can be made larger or smaller depending on the demands of the occasion, whether it be a full-blooded buffet meal or a cockail party where bite-sized treats are more appropriate.

In any case, the cornet is a simple and savoury item. The basic requirement is thin cooked ham slices, which you then use as they are or divide into smaller slices as you wish. Form these into a cone shape and secure with a cocktail stick.

The filling could be made from diced cooked chicken or turkey in mayonnaise, incorporating various additions for extra flavour and interest. Chopped black olives, capers, anchovies, peeled, deseeded and chopped red peppers, walnuts, chopped miniature gherkins, or snipped chives are only a few of the possibilities.

A more substantial variation on this theme would be to fill the cornets with cream cheese, lightened with whipped cream, to which again you add your own extras.

BACON AND LETTUCE PITTAS
FILLS 8 SMALL PITTA BREADS

12 oz/350 g streaky bacon, chopped
5 oz/150 g crisp young lettuce
3 good tablespoons mayonnaise, or more to taste
French mustard
freshly ground black pepper

Grill or fry the bacon in a non-stick pan, until crisp. Allow to cool. Break the lettuce into small pieces and divide between the pitta pockets. Stir the bacon into the mayonnaise and add mustard if you wish, finally seasoning to taste with black pepper.

Note Always warm up pitta bread, if you can, before using it; it is not half as satisfactory cold.

Bacon and egg raised pie (page 63), courgette salad (page 126),
bacon and lettuce pittas, and quick bacon bread (page 140)

HAM TARTLETS
MAKES 24

12 oz/350 g made shortcrust pastry (see page 142)
a little flour
10 oz/275 g soft cream cheese
5 tablespoons single cream
2 oz/50 g finely chopped spring onion
6 oz/175 g ham, minced or finely chopped
salt and black pepper
chopped chives or parsley, or sliced stuffed olives, for garnish

On a lightly floured surface, roll out the pastry dough as thinly as possible. Place 24 tartlet tins measuring about 2 in/5 cm across close together on a baking sheet. Roll the pastry on to a rolling pin, then unroll it over the tins. Using a small ball of floured pastry, gently press the pastry into the tins, then roll the rolling pin over the top to cut off the excess pastry. Place another tartlet tin into each (this will hold the pastry in position when cooking later) and chill for 10 minutes or so.

Bake the tartlet shells in a hot oven, 220°C/425°F/Gas Mark 7, for 7 minutes or so. Remove from the oven, allow to cool a little then transfer to a wire rack.

Make the filling by blending together the cream cheese and single cream and adding in the other ingredients, seasoning to taste. Divide this among the cooked tartlet shells. Decorate as you wish with one of the suggested garnishes before serving.

TARTLETS FILLED WITH SCRAMBLED EGG AND BACON
MAKES 24

24 pastry tartlet shells, prepared and cooked as in the preceding recipe
6 eggs scrambled in 2 oz/50 g butter
6 oz/175 g crisply fried bacon
fresh chopped parsley

Crumble the bacon and mix it into the scrambled eggs. Fill the tartlets with this mixture and garnish with chopped parsley. *See frontispiece*

PERFECT PARTNERS
VEGETABLES, SALADS & FRUITS

Bacon must be the most versatile meat because it goes with every kind of vegetable and fruit. This means that bacon dishes are infinitely variable, even when the bacon or ham is cooked simply, because there is a huge range of root and green vegetables, exotic imports such as peppers and aubergines, every kind of potato dish, all types of salads, and fruit for garnishes and sauces.

VEGETABLES

In the winter, white cabbage of all kinds, red cabbage and Brussels sprouts, and the old-fashioned kale are all natural partners of bacon, and their flavour will be very special if cooked in the liquid around the bacon joint. In the spring, there are spring greens and broccoli to enjoy, and cauliflowers and calabrese which are available throughout the year.

All the root vegetables go well with bacon, so you can choose from carrots, turnips, swedes and parsnips, as well as the onion family, including the mild-flavoured leek. The delectable summer vegetables like broad beans, peas, spinach, French beans and runner beans are all perfect with bacon, and nothing can be nicer than plainly grilled bacon or a slice of boiled bacon or ham with these early vegetables plainly dressed with a knob of butter and a few fresh herbs.

Peppers, aubergines, courgettes, mushrooms and tomatoes may be simply cooked in bacon fat, or filled with a bacon stuffing. Braised celery and chicory may be cooked in the oven alongside a bacon dish, while all the popular dried peas and beans are traditional accompaniments to salted meats.

POTATOES baked in their jackets may be cooked in the oven while a bacon dish is on another shelf, and their floury texture is very good as a contrast (bacon can be used as a filling for them too). New potatoes in season are good with plainly cooked bacon and summer vegetables, and as the potatoes grow older, they can be turned into creamy mashed potatoes, croquettes and chips which are perfect with grills and fry-ups.

SALADS Because bacon goes so well with both vegetables and fruit, accompanying salads can be very varied. For green stuff, we can use finely shredded white cabbage, lettuce, radicchio, Chinese leaves, chicory and watercress. In winter, there can be a mixture of chopped celery, slices of eating apples, orange segments and nuts. For a party, add pieces of pineapple and grapes, plums or cherries.

FRUIT

Citrus fruit may be used in salads, or slices may be used as garnish for a ham; halved oranges filled with cranberries make a particularly colourful garnish, or cranberries may be used for a garnish on their own or as a sauce. Apples are another good accompaniment, as a sauce, or as fried apple rings, or in salad. Sweet grapes, cherries and plums may be used in salads, while colourful pineapple rings, peach halves or apricot halves have a refreshing flavour to contrast with the meat. Grill these with a sprinkling of brown sugar and a few flakes of butter.

WINE AND OTHER DRINKS

Bacon is always slightly salty, and the accompaniments are often highly flavoured, and these can spoil the appreciation of fine wine. Cooked ham has a sweeter flavour and is more easily paired with wines for a celebration meal. It is a good partner for Beaujolais, Burgundy or Chianti, but the bottles should be good everyday ones, not fine vintages. A glass of dry sherry goes well before a bacon meal, and madeira or port are acceptable afterwards, and may also be used for accompanying sauces.

Cider and beer go extremely well with bacon, and may also be used for cooking the meat. Medium or dry cider, still or sparkling, is fine, and so are lager, ale or stout. Among the non-alcoholic drinks orange juice and apple juice are particularly good.

BROAD BEANS WITH PARSLEY SAUCE
SERVES 4

1 lb/450 g shelled broad beans
$\frac{1}{2}$ pint/300 ml parsley sauce (see page 128)
2 oz/50 g cooked ham, chopped
1 tablespoon chopped fresh parsley

Cook the beans in boiling salted water until just tender. Drain very well. Heat the parsley sauce and stir in the ham. Simmer for 2 minutes. Put the beans into a serving dish. Pour over the sauce and sprinkle with parsley.

LEEKS IN CHEESE SAUCE
SERVES 4

6 medium leeks
salt
1 pint/600 ml cheese sauce (see page 128)
pinch of ground nutmeg
1 oz/25 g fresh white breadcrumbs
1 oz/25 g grated Parmesan cheese

Clean the leeks very thoroughly and cut them into $\frac{1}{2}$ in/1.25 cm slices. Cook in boiling salted water until just tender. Drain very well, pressing out excess moisture. Mix the leeks into the cheese sauce and add nutmeg.

Place the mixture in an ovenware dish. Mix the breadcrumbs and cheese and sprinkle over the surface. Bake at 180°C/350°F/Gas Mark 4 for 25 minutes. Serve hot.

SOUTHERN BAKED BEANS
SERVES 4

8 oz/225 g haricot beans, soaked
1 pint/600 ml water
1 large onion, finely chopped
2 celery sticks, chopped
1 red pepper, chopped
4 tomatoes, skinned and chopped
1 tablespoon black treacle
1 tablespoon concentrated tomato purée
1 tablespoon wine vinegar
2 tablespoons Worcestershire sauce
2 teaspoons mustard powder
salt and pepper

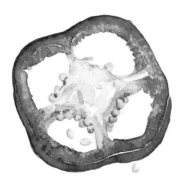

Soak the beans overnight and drain well. Cover with the fresh water, bring to the boil, cover and simmer for 1 hour. Drain and reserve $\frac{1}{2}$ pint/300 ml cooking liquid. Mix the onion, celery, pepper and tomatoes. Arrange the beans in alternating layers with the vegetables in a casserole. Mix the cooking liquid with the treacle, tomato purée, wine vinegar, sauce, mustard, salt and pepper. Pour into the casserole. Cover and bake at 180°C/350°F/Gas Mark 4 for $1\frac{1}{2}$ hours. Serve hot.

THREE BEAN SALAD
SERVES 4–6

8 oz/225 g red kidney beans, soaked
8 oz/225 g flageolet beans, soaked
8 oz/225 g haricot beans, soaked
1 medium onion, finely chopped
9 tablespoons oil
3 tablespoons red wine vinegar
pinch of mustard powder
salt and pepper
1 tablespoon chopped fresh parsley

Soak the beans overnight, and drain well. Put into separate pans with fresh water and boil until tender but unbroken. Drain very well and mix the beans in a salad bowl. Sprinkle with the onion. Mix the oil, vinegar, mustard, salt and pepper and pour over the beans. Sprinkle with parsley.

To save time, use canned beans, draining them very thoroughly before use.

AUSTRIAN LENTIL SALAD
SERVES 4

1 lb/450 g lentils, soaked
3 pints/1.8 l water
2 bay leaves
1 large onion
4 cloves
6 spring onions, finely chopped
4 oz/100 g dill pickled cucumbers, finely chopped
5 tablespoons olive oil
3 tablespoons red wine vinegar
$\frac{1}{2}$ teaspoon mustard powder
$\frac{1}{2}$ teaspoon paprika
salt and pepper
2 tablespoons chopped fresh parsley

Drain the lentils and put into a pan with the water, bay leaves and onion stuck with cloves. Bring to the boil, then cover and simmer until the lentils are just tender but not mushy. Drain well and discard bay leaves, onion and cloves.

Put the lentils into a bowl with the spring onions and cucumbers and mix well. Mix the oil, vinegar, mustard, paprika, salt and pepper. Pour over the lentils and toss lightly. Sprinkle with parsley and serve just warm.

BACON-STUFFED PEPPERS
SERVES 4

8 oz/225 g streaky or back bacon, diced finely
3 oz/75 g butter
1 medium onion, finely chopped
3 oz/75 g cooked rice
salt and black pepper
2 oz/50 g mushrooms, chopped
4 red or green peppers

Fry the bacon in a pan – non-stick preferably – for 2–3 minutes. Add 2 oz/50 g of the butter and the onion and continue frying until the bacon is very crisp and the onion is soft. Mix in the rest of the stuffing ingredients.

While the bacon is cooking, prepare the peppers. Cut a slice from the top, remove the core and seeds and blanch for 5 minutes in boiling salted water. Drain carefully.

Fill the peppers with the stuffing, replace the lids and brush with the rest of the butter, melted. Place in a shallow ovenproof dish and bake in a moderate oven, 180°C/350°F/Gas Mark 4, for about 25 minutes until the peppers are cooked. *Photographed on page 121*

PEASE PUDDING
SERVES 4

1 lb/450 g split peas, soaked
salt and pepper · 2 oz/50 g butter
2 eggs

Soak the peas overnight and drain well. Cover with fresh cold water and bring to the boil. Cover and simmer for 2 hours until the peas are very soft, and drain well. Mash the peas and season highly with salt and pepper. Beat in the butter and eggs.

Put the mixture into a greased pudding basin, cover and simmer in a covered pan of boiling water for 1 hour. Turn out and serve in slices. If preferred, put the mixture into a greased pie dish and bake at 180°C/350°F/Gas Mark 4 for 40 minutes.

VEGETABLE PURÉES
SERVES 4

Peas, beans, green vegetables and root vegetables make excellent purées. The flavour of the vegetables is very subtle when mixed with butter and cream and a little spice or some herbs.

1 lb/450 g prepared vegetables
2 oz/50 g butter
salt and pepper
6 tablespoons double cream
pinch of nutmeg *or* 1 teaspoon fresh herbs

Cook the vegetables in salted water until tender. Drain well, pressing out excess moisture. Put into a blender or food processor with butter, salt and pepper and blend to a smooth purée. Return to the pan and reheat very gently, adding the cream gradually. Flavour with appropriate spice or herb, and serve hot.

PEAS Flavour with mint
BROAD BEANS Flavour with summer savoury
BRUSSELS SPROUTS Flavour with nutmeg *Photographed on page 121*
SWEDE OR PARSNIPS Flavour with nutmeg
CARROT Flavour with cumin

CELERIAC AND PARSLEY PURÉE
SERVES 4

$1\frac{1}{2}$ lb/675 g celeriac
3–4 oz/75–100 g fresh parsley, stalks removed
$\frac{1}{4}$ pint/150 ml milk
salt and pepper

Peel the celeriac and cut it into chunks. Put into a pan of boiling salted water and cook for 10 minutes. Add the prepared parsley and cook for another 5 minutes, or until the celeriac is tender. Drain and put through a sieve or *mouli-legumes* (a blender or processor is likely to turn the mixture gluey). Return to a clean pan and reheat, with the milk. Season to taste and serve. *Photographed on page 121*

CHICORY WITH HAM AND A CHEESE SAUCE
SERVES 6

6 fat heads of chicory, trimmed, and hard core removed
$1\frac{1}{2}$ oz/40 g butter
salt and pepper
a pinch of sugar
6 thin slices cooked ham
French mustard
$\frac{1}{2}$ pint/300 ml cheese sauce (*see* page 128)
1 oz/25 g extra grated Parmesan or Gruyère cheese
1 oz/25 g breadcrumbs

Prepare the chicory and melt 1 oz/25 g of the butter in a heavy-based saucepan. Put in the chicory spears, salt and pepper and a pinch of sugar. Cover and leave to cook over a gentle heat for 40 minutes. The chicory is ready when a sharp-pointed knife pierces them easily. This is the best way of cooking chicory for the slow absorption of butter enhances its natural flavour. If you are pressed for time, however, you can simply blanch the chicory for 10 minutes in boiling salted water with a squeeze of lemon juice and a pinch of sugar. Drain when ready and press out excess moisture.

Whichever method you choose, continue by using the rest of the butter to grease a shallow ovenproof dish. Spread a little mustard over each slice of ham and wrap it around a spear of chicory. Then place them, overlapping side down, in the dish. Pour over the cheese sauce, scatter with the extra cheese and the breadcrumbs and bake in a moderately hot oven, 200°C/400°F/Gas Mark 6, for about 20 minutes. When it is ready it should be golden-brown and bubbling. Check how it is getting along after 10 minutes; if it seems to be slow in coming to this stage, turn up the oven to 220°C/425°F/Gas Mark 7 for the last stage of cooking.

Chicory with ham and a cheese sauce, bacon-stuffed peppers (page 118),
stuffed cabbage leaves Limoges style (page 123), and a trio of vegetables purees:
celeriac and parsley, carrot, and brussels sprout (page 119)

CREAMED SPINACH
SERVES 6

3 lb/1.5 kg fresh spinach *or* 2 lb/1 kg pack frozen leaf spinach
salt and black pepper
ground nutmeg
a little lemon juice
about 3 tablespoons double or whipping cream, or crème fraîche

First of all, if using fresh spinach, pick it over and remove and discard any withered leaves and tough stalks. Then wash it in several changes of cold water.

Continue by putting the washed fresh spinach – or the frozen straight from its pack – into a large saucepan. No water needs to be added in either case; sufficient clings to the leaves to make this unnecessary. Sprinkle with salt, cover tightly and cook over a low heat for 5 minutes or so. At the end of that time, stir well and raise the heat so that the liquid evaporates and the vegetable cooks more quickly. When tender, drain in a colander, cut roughly, press a small plate down on it to get rid of as much moisture as possible, then leave to drain.

When ready to serve, return the spinach to its pan, stir over a good heat to evaporate any remaining moisture, then mix in the seasonings and enough cream to make a smooth, unifying sauce.

GLAZED CARROT STICKS
SERVES 6

$1\frac{1}{2}$ lb/675 g carrots
2 teaspoons granulated sugar
$\frac{3}{4}$ oz/20 g butter
$\frac{1}{2}$ teaspoon salt · pinch of white pepper

Peel the carrots and cut them into 'matchstick' pieces, about 2 in/5 cm long and $\frac{1}{8}$ in/$\frac{1}{4}$ cm thick. Put the prepared carrots into a saucepan with a very little water – just enough to keep them from catching on the bottom – the sugar, butter, salt and white pepper. Cover tightly and cook over a gentle heat until just tender. Check the seasoning and serve; the liquid should have evaporated to form a glaze over the carrots.

If you are lucky enough to have small, young carrots straight from the garden, they can simply be topped and tailed and left whole for cooking in this way.

STUFFED CABBAGE LEAVES LIMOGES STYLE
SERVES 6–8

The simplest of the stuffed cabbage leaf recipes, from one of the great chestnut districts of France, is the best. The combination of crispness, softness and piquancy is perfectly balanced. It makes a good supper dish, or first course, and the small cabbage rolls can be used to decorate and enhance a roast chicken or turkey.

36 cabbage leaves
$1\frac{1}{2}$ lb/675 g chestnuts, fresh or 12 oz/350 g dried
12 rashers smoked streaky bacon
good 4 oz/125 g butter

Soak the dried chestnuts overnight, then cook them. If using fresh, simply peel them. Blanch the cabbage leaves in boiling salted water for 2 minutes, then drain and pat them dry. Spread out the blanched leaves and divide the chestnuts between them (it does not matter if they have broken up a little). Cut the bacon into 36 pieces and lay them on top. Roll up and place closely together in a large pan in layers. Pour in enough water to come within $\frac{1}{2}$ in/1 cm of the top. Dot with a third of the butter, put a plate on top and cover. Bring to the boil and simmer for 25 minutes. Remove the lid so that the liquid evaporates to a smallish amount of juice – a further 10 minutes.

Place the rolls on a dish or around the bird. Whisk the remaining butter into the pan juices and then pour it over the cabbage rolls.

At Christmas time the rolls can be prepared the previous day and kept in the refrigerator until an hour before the meal.

Note The bacon provides enough salt.

Photographed on page 121

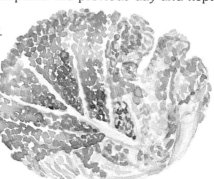

CARROT AND SPINACH MOUSSES
SERVES 6

12 oz/350 g carrots, thinly sliced
13 tablespoons crème fraîche*
2 egg whites, whisked to soft peaks
12 oz/350 g fresh spinach *or* 8 oz/225 g frozen *leaf* spinach
freshly ground nutmeg
salt and freshly ground black pepper

Cook the carrots in a very small amount of water in a covered saucepan until tender – if they are really thinly sliced this will take only 5 minutes. Drain and purée with 5 tablespoons crème fraîche. Season to taste with salt and pepper and fold in half the whisked egg white.

Cook the spinach, whether fresh or frozen, without any extra water until tender. Drain and press out excess liquid. Purée with 8 tablespoons crème fraiche and season to taste with nutmeg and salt and pepper. Fold in the rest of the whisked egg white.

Divide the carrot purée between 6 individual moulds or ramekin dishes. Tap them lightly on the work surface to level the purée. Top with the spinach and level off with the back of a knife.

Cover the moulds or ramekins with foil and cook, in a baking tin filled with enough hot water to come half-way up their sides, in a moderate oven, 180°C/350°F/Gas Mark 4, for 25–30 minutes until the mousses are just firm to the touch.

Leave to cool a little, then invert on to a serving dish or individual plates. *Photographed on page 83*

*See note about crème fraîche on page 77.

CELERIAC IN MUSTARD SAUCE
SERVES 6

1 celeriac, weighing about 1 lb/450 g
vinegar
salt and pepper
juice of 1 lemon
2 tablespoons French mustard
$\frac{1}{2}$ pint/300 ml lightly whipped double cream, *or* mayonnaise
chopped parsley

Peel the celeriac root, cutting away any dark patches. Cut it into julienne (matchstick) pieces with a knife, or put it through the shredding blade of a food processor or *mouli-julienne*, putting it as you do so into a bowl of water acidulated with 1 tablespoon vinegar to 2 pints/1 litre. This is to prevent the celeriac from discolouring. When it is all ready, bring more acidulated water to a boil, tip in the celeriac for just as long as it takes for the water to return to the boil. Then drain in a colander and refresh under cold running water. This short blanching takes away any 'woodiness' from the vegetable yet still leaves it crisp.

To finish, mix the salt and pepper, lemon juice and mustard together and stir them into the cream or mayonnaise. Check the seasoning, turn the celeriac well in this dressing, transfer to a serving dish and sprinkle with parsley. *Photographed on page 131*

CHICORY SALAD
SERVES 6

3 heads chicory, trimmed
2 oz/50 g shelled walnuts, coarsely chopped
3 oz/75 g Edam or mild Cheddar cheese, diced
1 red pepper, deseeded and very thinly sliced in rings
1 tablespoon freshly chopped parsley
French dressing, mayonnaise or cream flavoured with French mustard and lemon juice

Carefully remove the leaves from the chicory, but leave the little cores at the centre whole.
Mix all the salad ingredients with enough dressing to coat lightly, chill and serve.

COURGETTE SALAD
SERVES 4

8 medium courgettes
1 medium onion, finely chopped
1 garlic clove, finely chopped
6 tablespoons oil
2 tablespoons white wine vinegar
crisp lettuce leaves or radicchio
1 tablespoon capers
1 teaspoon chopped fresh parsley
1 teaspoon chopped fresh marjoram
salt and pepper

Wash and dry the courgettes and cut them into $\frac{1}{2}$in/1.25 cm slices without peeling. Put into a pan of boiling salted water and simmer for 10 minutes. Drain well and put into a bowl with the onion and garlic. Mix the oil and vinegar and pour over. Leave to stand for 2 hours.

Arrange a bed of lettuce or radicchio on a serving dish. Drain the courgettes, retaining the liquid, and put the courgettes, onion and garlic on the leaves. Mix the liquid with the capers, herbs, salt and pepper. Pour over courgettes. Chill before serving. *Photographed on page 111*

ORANGE SALAD
SERVES 4

4 large oranges · crisp lettuce leaves
watercress sprigs · 4 tablespoons oil
2 tablespoons white wine vinegar
salt and pepper · pinch of sugar

Remove 4 strips of orange peel from the oranges. Strip off any white pith and cut the peel in very fine shreds. Blanch in boiling water for 1 minute and drain very well. Peel the oranges and remove all white pith. Cut oranges across in very thin slices and discard pips.

Arrange a bed of lettuce leaves on a serving dish and place sliced oranges on top with any juice which has run out of them. Garnish with watercress sprigs. Mix with oil and vinegar and season with salt, pepper and sugar. Pour over the oranges and sprinkle with orange peel shreds. Chill for 30 minutes before serving.

VEGETABLES, SALADS & FRUIT

SIDE EFFECTS
SAUCES, RELISHES,
STUFFINGS, BREADS & PASTRY

A sauce or relish or unusual bread can make a tremendous difference to the presentation of a dish. Because bacon and ham are so versatile, there is no problem about choosing suitable accompaniments, prepared with fruit, herbs and spices. Most of the appropriate sauces can be made quickly for instant use, but it is worth spending time to make some special treats such as spiced fruit which will keep for emergency use. Bacon itself can provide an attractive stuffing for vegetables, but fruit stuffings are ideal for bacon joints.

BASIC WHITE SAUCE
MAKES $\frac{1}{2}$ pint/300 ml SAUCE

1 oz/25 g butter
1 oz/25 g plain flour
$\frac{1}{2}$ pint/300 ml milk
salt and pepper

Put the butter into a small pan and melt over low heat. Work in the flour and cook for 1 minute. Remove from the heat and gradually stir in the milk. Return to the heat and cook gently, stirring well, until the sauce is smooth and creamy. Season to taste with salt and pepper.

PARSLEY SAUCE Add 1 tablespoon chopped fresh parsley.
EGG SAUCE Add 2 finely chopped hard-boiled eggs.
CAPER SAUCE Add 2 oz/50 g chopped capers.
CHEESE SAUCE Remove sauce from heat and stir in 3 oz/75 g grated Cheddar cheese. Stir until melted and add a pinch of mustard powder.
CURRY SAUCE Cook 1 finely chopped small onion in the butter, until soft and golden. Add 2 teaspoons curry powder and cook for 1 minute before adding flour and milk.

CRANBERRY SAUCE
SERVES 4—6

8 oz/225 g fresh cranberries
2 oz/50 g sugar
$\frac{1}{4}$ pint/150 ml water

Wash the berries and drain well. Put the sugar and water into a pan and heat gently until the sugar has dissolved. Add the berries and continue simmering until they pop, which will take about 10 minutes. Do not overcook or the sauce will have a mushy texture. Put into a serving dish and serve cold. *Photographed on page 97*

CUMBERLAND SAUCE
MAKES $\frac{1}{2}$ pint/300 ml

1 orange
1 small lemon
1 shallot, finely chopped
8 oz/225 g redcurrant jelly
1 teaspoon Dijon mustard
4 fl oz/100 ml tawny port
a pinch of ground ginger
cayenne pepper
salt

Carefully peel the zest from the orange and lemon, leaving behind the white pith. Cut the zest into needle-thin julienne strips and blanch them by boiling in water for 2 minutes. Drain and reserve the strips, together with the squeezed juice of the orange and lemon.

Blanch the shallot also in boiling water, for 4 minutes, and drain.

Put the redcurrant jelly into a saucepan with the orange and lemon juices and heat gently until melted. Stir in the shallots, mustard, port, ginger and citrus zest and simmer together for 3 minutes. Season to taste with cayenne pepper and salt – it should need only a little of either as the sauce is piquant as it is. Serve cold.

Cumberland sauce keeps well in the refrigerator, covered.

CHERRY WALNUT RELISH
SERVES 4

8 oz/225 g ripe black cherries
2 oz/50 g chopped walnuts
4 tablespoons oil
2 tablespoons white wine vinegar
salt and pepper
2 tablespoons double cream

Stone the cherries and put into a serving bowl. Sprinkle on the walnuts. Mix the oil, vinegar, salt and pepper, and pour over the cherries. Leave to stand for 1 hour. Just before serving, pour on the cream and serve at once.

If liked canned cherries may be used, but they must be very well drained.

PLUM AND TARRAGON RELISH
SERVES 4

1 lb/450 g ripe eating plums
6 tablespoons oil
2 tablespoons red wine vinegar
salt and pepper
pinch of sugar
1 tablespoon chopped fresh tarragon

Wash and dry the plums. Split them in half and discard the stones, then slice. Put into a serving bowl. Mix the oil, vinegar, salt, pepper and sugar and pour over the plums. Chill for 1 hour. Stir well and sprinkle with tarragon.

Sliced ham with, *from the top left*, celeriac in mustard sauce (page 125), cherry walnut relish, spiced pears (page 133), plum and tarragon relish, and green mayonnaise (overleaf)

SAUCES, RELISHES, STUFFINGS, BREADS & PASTRY

MAYONNAISE
MAKES $\frac{1}{2}$ pint/300 ml

2 egg yolks
$\frac{1}{2}$ teaspoon salt
$\frac{1}{2}$ teaspoon mustard powder
$\frac{1}{4}$ teaspoon pepper
$\frac{1}{2}$ pint/300 ml olive oil
1 tablespoon lemon juice or wine vinegar

Put the egg yolks, salt, mustard and pepper into a bowl and mix together with a wooden spoon. Add the oil drop by drop, beating all the time, until the oil has been completely absorbed. Add the lemon juice or vinegar. Keep in a cool place, but do not chill.

A herb-flavoured vinegar may be used for variety. For a lighter mayonnaise, salad oil may be used instead of olive oil.

BLENDER MAYONNAISE Substitute 1 whole egg for the egg yolks. Blend the egg, seasonings and lemon juice or vinegar for 5 seconds, and then gradually add the oil while the machine is running. The mayonnaise will be ready in about 1 minute. The same method may be used with a food processor.

GREEN MAYONNAISE Blend together 1 garlic clove, a tablespoon fresh parsley, 1 tablespoon fresh dill and 1 tablespoon fresh chives, and stir into the mayonnaise. *Photographed on page 131*

SWEDISH MAYONNAISE This is a good variation on the mayonnaise theme for cold ham: simply add an equal quantity of cold apple purée (see the recipe for apple sauce, page 137) to the mayonnaise; flavour it to taste with grated or creamed horseradish.

SPICED PEARS
MAKES 2 lb/900 g

2 lb/900 g small cooking pears
8 oz/225 g sugar
8 oz/225 g white vinegar
small piece of root ginger
small piece of cinnamon stick
2 teaspoons allspice
small piece of lemon rind
cloves

Peel and core the pears and cut them in half. Put into a pan, just cover with water and simmer for 20 minutes. Drain very well.

Put the sugar and vinegar into a pan. Tie the ginger, cinnamon stick, allspice and lemon rind in a piece of muslin and suspend in the pan. Bring to the boil. Stick a clove into each piece of pear and add the pears to the vinegar. Simmer until the pears are tender and beginning to look transparent. Lift the pears into clean hot preserving jars with a slotted spoon. Boil the syrup until it thickens slightly. Pour over the pears and seal tightly. Store in a cool place for 1–2 weeks before serving. *Photographed on page 131*

SPICED PEACHES
SERVES 6

12 canned peach halves in syrup
4 oz/100 g sugar
6 tablespoons cider vinegar
grated rind of 1 orange
3 in/7.5 cm cinnamon stick
6 cloves · 4 allspice berries

Drain the peaches but reserve $\frac{1}{4}$ pint/150 ml syrup. Put the syrup into a pan with the sugar, vinegar, orange rind and spices. Bring to the boil and add the peach halves. Simmer uncovered for 5 minutes. Pour into a bowl, cover and leave to cool to room temperature. Lift the peaches into a serving bowl and strain the liquid over them. Chill before serving. *Photographed on page 97*

MADEIRA SAUCE
MAKES $\frac{1}{2}$ pint/300 ml

$\frac{1}{2}$ pint/300 ml brown stock
1 tablespoon arrowroot
1 tablespoon each finely chopped carrot, onion and celery
1 tablespoon finely chopped ham or bacon
4 tablespoons Madeira
1 tablespoon softened butter
salt and pepper

Bring the brown stock to boil. Mix the arrowroot with 2 tablespoons cold water to make a paste. Add this to the stock, whisking constantly, until the sauce is thick enough to coat lightly the back of a spoon. Add the prepared vegetables, ham or bacon and 2 tablespoons of the Madeira and simmer together for 15 minutes. Strain the sauce, return to a clean pan, add the rest of the Madeira, and reheat. Just before serving, whisk in the butter. Check the seasoning and pour into a warmed sauce boat. *Photographed on page 97*

APRICOT SAUCE
MAKES $\frac{1}{2}$ pint/300 ml

4 oz/100 g dried apricots
$\frac{1}{2}$ pint/300 ml water, plus 2 teaspoonsful
1 tablespoon honey
1 teaspoon arrowroot or cornflour
3 tablespoons brandy
2 pieces preserved stem ginger, finely diced

Put the apricots into a saucepan, cover with the $\frac{1}{2}$ pint/300 ml water, add the honey and simmer for 5 minutes or until tender. Drain, and reserve the liquid.

Cream the arrowroot or cornflour with the 2 teaspoons water, add to the poaching liquid and cook gently, stirring, until it thickens and clears. Put into a blender and purée with the apricots.

Return the sauce to its pan, add the cognac and ginger and heat through.

TOMATO SAUCE
MAKES $\frac{1}{2}$ pint/300 ml

2 shallots, finely chopped
1 carrot, finely chopped
1 garlic clove, finely chopped
1 oz/25 g butter or 2 tablespoons olive oil
1 tablespoon plain flour
$\frac{1}{4}$ pint/150 ml stock or dry white wine
1 lb/450 g ripe tomatoes *or* 14 oz/400 g can Italian peeled plum tomatoes
bouquet garni: parsley sprigs, sprig of thyme, small bay leaf, few peppercorns, tied in muslin
pinch of sugar
1 tablespoon concentrated tomato purée
salt and pepper
wine vinegar (optional)

Cook the shallots, carrrot and garlic gently in the butter or oil until the vegetables are soft but not browned. Sprinkle in the flour, and stir for a couple of minutes, then remove from the heat and stir in the stock or wine.

Add the tomatoes – quartered if they are fresh, just as they are if canned – the bouquet garni and flavourings, except for the vinegar. Simmer, uncovered, for 1 hour.

If you would like a smooth sauce, push the sauce through a sieve, pressing down hard on the vegetables to extract all the goodness, into a clean pan. Bring to a boil and reduce over a moderate heat, if necessary, to thicken it to the consistency of double cream.

Taste, and adjust the seasoning, adding a little wine vinegar at this stage if you wish. If you have used fresh tomatoes they may need rather more seasoning. *Photographed on page 69*

RÉMOULADE SAUCE
MAKES $\frac{1}{2}$ pint/300 ml

Basic mayonnaise recipe (page 132), made by hand
1 tablespoon French mustard
3 tablespoons chopped capers
3 tablespoons chopped fresh herbs
3 tablespoons chopped gherkins

Beat the mustard into the mayonnaise, stir in the
capers and herbs and check the seasoning
before serving with cold ham.

SCANDINAVIAN MUSTARD SAUCE
MAKES 12 fl oz/350 ml

2 tablespoons brown sugar
3 tablespoons malt vinegar
2 fl oz/50 ml prepared mustard
2 egg yolks
8 fl oz/250 ml oil
3 tablespoons chopped fresh dill weed or $1\frac{1}{2}$ tablespoons dried
salt and pepper to taste

In a small bowl, whisk together the sugar, vinegar, mustard and egg yolks. Slowly add the oil,
as for mayonnaise, until the mixture begins to thicken. Then add the oil in a steady stream,
whisking constantly. Stir in the dill weed and taste for seasoning. (*Note*: the sauce should taste
of mustard but should not be overpowering.)
   The sauce may be stored in the refrigerator for up to a week. Serve it at room temperature.

APPLE SAUCE
SERVES 4–6

1 lb/450 g cooking apples
2 oz/50 g sugar
1 oz/25 g butter
pinch of ground cloves or cinnamon

Use apples which become soft and fluffy when cooked. Peel and core and slice thinly into a pan. Just cover with water and simmer until the apples have collapsed and formed a purée. Add the sugar, butter and spice and beat well. Serve hot or cold.

CIDER APPLE SAUCE Use dry cider instead of water. If liked, stir in a few seedless raisins.

WATERCRESS SAUCE
MAKES $\frac{1}{2}$ pint/300 ml SAUCE

2 bunches watercress
$\frac{1}{4}$ pint/150 ml water
1 oz/25 g butter
1 oz/25 g plain flour
$\frac{1}{2}$ pint/300 ml milk
salt and pepper
pinch of ground nutmeg

Remove the leaves from one bunch of watercress and keep on one side. Cut off the thick stems from the second bunch and discard. Put the leaves and thin stems into the water and simmer for 10 minutes until the water has almost evaporated. Push through a sieve and keep on one side.

Melt the butter over low heat and work in the flour. Cook for 1 minute. Remove from the heat and gradually stir in the milk. Return to the heat and cook gently, stirring well, until the sauce is smooth and creamy. Add the watercress purée and continue cooking for 2 minutes. Chop the reserved watercress leaves very finely. Stir into the sauce and season with salt, pepper and nutmeg. Serve hot.

BARBECUE RELISH
MAKES 1 pint/600 ml

1 onion, finely chopped
1 oz/25 g butter
1 tablespoon oil
grated rind of 1 lemon
14 oz/400 g can of tomatoes
pinch of sugar
1 green pepper, chopped
2 oz/50 g mushrooms, chopped
1 teaspoon brown sugar
few drops of Tabasco
pinch of mixed herbs
salt and pepper

Cook the onion in butter and oil without browning for 5 minutes. Stir in the remaining ingredients, bring them to the boil, then reduce the heat and simmer for 30–35 minutes.

Serve with grilled or fried gammon steaks or bacon chops.

RAISIN SAUCE
SERVES 4–6

4 oz/100 g seedless raisins
$\frac{1}{2}$ pint/300 ml water
2 oz/50 g dark soft brown sugar
1 tablespoon cornflour
pinch of salt
1 tablespoon wine vinegar
1 oz/25 g butter

Put the raisins into a pan. Reserve 2 tablespoons water and add the rest to the raisins. Simmer for 5 minutes. Mix the remaining water with the sugar, cornflour and salt. Stir into the raisins and simmer for 3 minutes. Stir in the vinegar and butter and serve hot.

APRICOT AND NUT STUFFING
FOR BACON
ENOUGH FOR 3 lb/1.35 kg BACON JOINT

4 oz/100 g dried apricots
8 oz/225 g day-old bread
2 celery sticks, chopped
2 oz/50 g chopped walnuts
2 oz/50 g melted butter
salt and pepper

Put the apricots into a pan and cover with water. Bring to the boil and simmer for 5 minutes. Leave to cool in the cooking liquid. Make the bread into crumbs and mix with the celery and walnuts. Chop the apricots finely and add to the breadcrumbs with 6 tablespoons cooking liquid. Stir in the melted butter and season well with salt and pepper.

RAISIN AND RICE STUFFING
FOR BACON
ENOUGH FOR 3 lb/1.35 kg BACON JOINT

1 oz/25 g butter
1 medium onion, finely chopped
4 oz/100 g long grain rice
2 oz/50 g seedless raisins
2 oz/50 g chopped almonds
grated rind of 1 orange
$\frac{1}{2}$ teaspoon Tabasco sauce
salt and pepper
1 egg, beaten

Melt the butter and cook the onion over low heat for 5 minutes until soft and golden. Cook the rice in boiling salted water for 6 minutes and drain well. Add the rice to the onion and mix in the raisins, almonds, orange rind, sauce, salt and pepper. Leave until completely cold and stir in the beaten egg.

BACON STUFFING FOR VEGETABLES
MAKES 8 oz/225 g STUFFING

4 oz/100 g white breadcrumbs
4 oz/100 g back bacon rashers, finely chopped
$\frac{1}{2}$ teaspoon mustard powder
$\frac{1}{2}$ teaspoon mixed fresh herbs
salt and pepper
1 oz/25 g melted butter
4 tablespoons milk

Put the breadcrumbs into a bowl and mix in the bacon, mustard, herbs, salt and pepper. Add the butter and milk and mix well.

QUICK BACON BREAD
MAKES 1 lb/450 g LOAF

4 back bacon rashers, finely chopped
1 oz/25 g butter
8 oz/225 g self-raising flour
$\frac{1}{2}$ teaspoon salt
pepper
2 celery sticks, finely chopped
1 teaspoon mixed fresh herbs
1 egg
$\frac{1}{4}$ pint/150 ml milk

Grease and base-line a 1 lb/450 g loaf tin. Cook the bacon in the butter until cooked but not crisp. Sieve the flour, salt and pepper together. Stir in the bacon and butter with celery and herbs. Beat the egg and milk together and work into the mixture. Spoon into the tin. Bake at 190°C/375°F/Gas Mark 5 for 45 minutes. Turn out and cool on a wire rack. Serve freshly baked, sliced and spread with butter. *Photographed on page 111*

WILTSHIRE BACON SCONES
MAKES 8

These scones make a delicious alternative to bread, served hot from the oven, spread thickly with butter at breakfast or tea time, or for lunch with a freshly-tossed mixed green salad.

4 oz/100 g streaky bacon, derinded and chopped
1 small onion, grated
4 sticks celery, chopped
1 lb/450 g self-raising flour
$\frac{1}{2}$ teaspoon mustard powder
$\frac{1}{4}$ teaspoon salt
black pepper
2 oz/50 g dripping
2 tablespoons chopped parsley
scant $\frac{1}{2}$ pint/300 ml milk
1 egg

Put the chopped bacon into a frying pan and heat for a couple of minutes, until the fat runs. Add the onion and chopped celery, fry for 5 minutes then allow to cool.

Sift together the flour, mustard powder, salt and pepper, and rub in the dripping until the mixture is like fine breadcrumbs. Add the parsley and stir in the bacon and vegetable mixture.

Beat together the milk and egg and stir into the flour. Knead the dough on a floured surface.

Grease a baking tray. Shape the dough on the tray into a round, and mark into 8 sections lightly with a knife.

Bake for 25 minutes in a hot oven, 200°C/400°F/Gas Mark 6. *Photographed on page 89*

SHORTCRUST PASTRY
MAKES 12 oz/350 g

8 oz/225 g plain flour · $\frac{1}{2}$ teaspoon salt
2 oz/50 g hard margarine
2 oz/50 g lard
2–3 tablespoons cold water

Sift together the flour and salt. Cut the fat into small pieces and rub into the flour until the mixture is like fine breadcrumbs. Add water and mix to a firm dough. Turn on to a floured board and knead quickly and lightly until smooth. Roll out to required shape and thickness.

PUFF PASTRY
MAKES $2\frac{1}{2}$ lb/1.25 kg

1 lb/450 g plain flour · 1 teaspoon salt
1 lb/450 g unsalted butter or hard margarine
2 teaspoons lemon juice
$\frac{1}{2}$ pint/300 ml less 1 tablespoon iced water

Sift together the flour and salt. Divide the fat into 4 equal pieces. Rub one quarter into the flour and mix to a pliable dough with lemon juice and water. Turn on to a floured board and knead until smooth. Leave to rest for 15 minutes in a cool place. With two knives, form the remaining fat into a slab 5 in/12.5 cm square on a floured board.

Roll dough into a 6 × 11 in/15 × 27.5 cm rectangle. Place the slab of fat on the top end of the dough, leaving a margin of about $\frac{1}{2}$ in/1.25 cm along the sides and top. Fold the rest of the dough over, placing upper edges of dough together. Brush off surplus flour.

First rolling Turn the pastry round so that the folded edge is on the left-hand side. Press three open edges together with rolling pin to seal. Press the dough across about 5 times with a rolling pin to flatten. Roll out to a 6 × 12 in/15 × 30 cm rectangle, keeping edges straight.

Second rolling Fold pastry in three by folding bottom third upwards and top third downwards and over to cover it. Turn so that folded edge is again on the left. Seal edges and roll out as before. Fold, turn and seal edges as before. Place the pastry on a floured plate in a polythene bag and leave to rest in a cold place for 20 minutes.

Third to sixth rollings Roll out 4 more times, always turning and sealing dough as before. Leave to rest 20 minutes in a cold place between each rolling. If any patches of fat still show, roll again. Rest dough finally before rolling out thinly and cutting to required shape.

INDEX

Page numbers in *italics* refer to photographs